60 no-fuss re...
with Maximum Flavor and Mi...

The Paleo Sheet Pan
COOKBOOK

JENNIFER BUMB

Founder of *Pretend It's a Donut*

PAGE STREET
PUBLISHING CO.

PAGE STREET
PUBLISHING CO.

Copyright © 2020 Jennifer Bumb
First published in 2020 by
Page Street Publishing Co.
27 Congress Street, Suite 105
Salem, MA 01970
www.pagestreetpublishing.com

Distributed by Macmillan, sales in Canada by The Canadian Manda Group.

24 23 22 21 20   1 2 3 4 5

ISBN-13: 978-1-64567-026-1
ISBN-10: 1-64567-026-0

Library of Congress Control Number: 2019951642

Cover and book design by Ashley Tenn for Page Street Publishing Co.
Photography by Jerod Muse

Printed and bound in China

Dedication

To my grandmother Audrey Gray, who, even in the face of adversity,
was perseverant, a constant source of inspiration and a woman
I truly wish everyone had gotten the chance to meet.

TABLE OF *Contents*

SIDES: AW, SHEET, HERE COME THE SIDES!   83

DESSERT: YOU DESERVE IT!   115

INTRODUCTION

Good health starts with good food, and these delicious, approachable sheet pan recipes use real, fresh ingredients to bring family and friends to the table.

Hi, everyone! My name is Jenn, and I'm the face behind the popular Paleo food blog Pretend It's a Donut. I grew up with a family that loved to cook, so it's always been something I've enjoyed doing. We never ate terribly, but never really thought about the foods that we were putting in our bodies and the negative effects some foods could have. It wasn't until after my fifth kid that I really realized how important my health and my family's health is. Not only physically, but mentally. So, we went Paleo and have never looked back!

I started the blog and an Instagram account to share recipes with my friends and family. The blog quickly grew to having 15,000 weekly readers, and the Instagram account has more than 70,000 followers. One thing led to another and, in 2016, I was lucky enough to be asked to contribute a couple of recipes to the first Whole30 cookbook.

As my kids started getting older, it became a little harder to make large quantities of food every night for us on the stovetop. So, I started tossing everything onto a sheet pan and cooking it up in the oven. Well . . . my family ate it up (literally and figuratively!). I was also able to be more present with them while the sheet pan meal was cooking in the oven. I then started sharing more sheet pan meals on my blog, and I even wrote a small e-cookbook called *One Pan Wonders: Paleo Meals That Are the Sheet*. I still longed to share even more easy, healthy sheet pan recipes with all of you, in a way that's right in your kitchen and at your fingertips. Thus, this cookbook was born!

There is something special about having an actual cookbook in your kitchen, with the pages dog-eared and food-splotched. Recipes in a cookbook aren't forgotten, and favorites are shared and made over and over again. I'm so excited for you to dig in to every single one of these sheet pan Paleo recipes, especially the Heavenly Blueberry Pancakes (page 18) and the Perfectly Baked Breakfast Taquitos (page 29) from the breakfast section or the Mini Sweet Potato Reuben Stacks (page 104) from the sides chapter. And don't even get me started on the Jalapeño-Popper Stuffed Chicken (page 42) and the Ooey-Gooey Avocado Brownies (page 120)! My mouth is watering just thinking about these scrumptious recipes.

With the way our world and our increasingly busy schedules are these days, it's no wonder our health has taken a back seat in our everyday lives. The thing is, making a Paleo-approved meal at home doesn't need to take that back seat. This book aims to make healthy eating fun and sustainable, with hands-off sheet pan meals that minimize your dishes and that are super easy as far as cleanup goes! And believe me, with seven mouths to feed, I'm all about keeping it simple and tasty.

Not to mention, these gluten-free, lactose-free and grain-free recipes sound and taste so good that it's hard to believe that they're Paleo and all cooked on a sheet pan! Are you drooling yet?

Breakfast
LET'S GET OUR SHEET TOGETHER!

Grab your cup o' Joe because we are about to talk breakfast! We all know it as the most important meal of the day, but we often forget to eat it. It's such a shame, because breakfast really does give you the energy you need to start your day. Especially when you are living that Paleo life, which is eating clean, wholesome foods with real ingredients and none of the sugary, processed breakfasts that give you a nasty feeling and major slump an hour after you finish eating.

What I love about these sheet pan breakfasts is that you don't need to babysit the food. Just toss everything together, place it onto the sheet pan, set the timer and go get yourself beautiful. Some of my favorites are the Perfectly Baked Breakfast Taquitos (page 29) and the Broccoli–Chicken Sausage Egg Tart (page 14).

PUMPKIN SPICE PANCAKES

Hurry up and get yourself to the nearest grocery store and pick up all the cans of pumpkin that you possibly can! You can get cans of pumpkin any time of the year, which is fantastic news for you and your family. Pumpkin is packed full of vitamins, and it is high in antioxidants, which have been known to reduce the risk of chronic diseases. These pancakes are best eaten right out of the oven with a drizzle of maple syrup.

SERVES 8

1⅓ cups (170 g) tapioca flour

3 cups (336 g) superfine almond flour

2 tsp (9 g) baking soda

1 tsp sea salt

1 tsp ground nutmeg

2 tsp (5 g) ground cinnamon

6 eggs

1 (15-oz [425-g]) can pumpkin

¼ cup (60 ml) honey

1 tbsp plus 1 tsp (20 ml) apple cider vinegar

1 tbsp plus 1 tsp (20 ml) vanilla extract

Maple syrup

Coconut cream, optional

Preheat the oven to 425°F (218°C). Line a baking sheet with parchment paper.

In a large bowl, mix together the tapioca flour, almond flour, baking soda, salt, nutmeg and cinnamon. Add in the eggs, pumpkin, honey, vinegar and vanilla. Whisk until well combined. Pour the batter onto the prepared baking sheet.

Bake the pancakes for 8 minutes, or until a toothpick inserted into the center comes out clean. Cut the pancakes into squares and top them with the maple syrup and the coconut cream, if using.

SWEET POTATO BENNIES

This dish is fresh, vibrant and not to be missed. Using sweet potatoes instead of bread makes for a fun and Paleo-friendly twist on the traditional benedict. You can keep it traditional by poaching the eggs, or let the oven do all the work and cook the eggs for you. Sweet potatoes are great to have in the morning, as they are filled with fiber and beta carotene, a fantastic antioxidant. Don't overthink the hollandaise: it really is very easy and completes this sweet potato benedict!

SERVES 8

FOR THE BENEDICT

2 sweet potatoes, each cut into 4 slices, lengthwise

8 pieces sugar-free bacon, sliced, optional

Handful of arugula

2 tomatoes, each cut into 4 slices

1 tbsp (15 ml) apple cider vinegar

8 eggs

FOR THE HOLLANDAISE SAUCE

½ cup (113 g) ghee

4 egg yolks

1 tbsp (15 ml) fresh lemon juice

1 tbsp (2 g) dried tarragon

1 tsp cayenne pepper

For the benedicts, preheat the oven to 400°F (204°C). Line a baking sheet with parchment paper.

Arrange the potato slices in the prepared pan to form the base of the benedict. If you are using the bacon, add a piece to each potato slice. Bake the potatoes for 10 minutes.

Remove the potatoes from the oven and top each benedict with a few pieces of the arugula and a tomato slice. (If you want to cook the eggs in the oven instead of poaching them, you can crack an egg onto each benedict after adding the tomato.) Return the pan to the oven and bake for another 10 minutes, or until the potatoes are fork tender.

Prepare the hollandaise while the benedicts finish cooking in the oven. Melt the ghee in a small pot over medium-low heat. Turn off the heat and, while whisking, add the egg yolks one at a time. If you go too quickly, you will scramble your eggs, so take your time. Whisk for about 2 minutes, until the mixture thickens. Add the lemon juice, tarragon and cayenne. Whisk until combined. You can be a bit generous with the cayenne, as it takes a lot to make it spicy.

To poach the eggs, bring a pot filled with 2 inches (5 cm) of water and the vinegar to a slow boil. Crack an egg into a small ramekin. Swirl the boiling water with a spoon. Carefully pour the egg into the spinning water and poach it for 2½ minutes, or until the egg starts to rise up from the bottom of the pot. Remove the egg with a slotted spoon, and transfer it to a plate. Cover the plate with foil to keep the egg warm. Repeat with the remaining eggs.

When the potatoes are cooked, transfer the benedicts to plates, and top them with the poached eggs. Drizzle the hollandaise sauce all over the top.

NOTE: If your hollandaise seems too thick, whisk in a tablespoon (15 ml) of warm water.

BROCCOLI–CHICKEN SAUSAGE EGG TART

Quiches or breakfast tarts are always first on my plate when I am at brunch or a party. The funny thing is that I usually only have them at events, and every time I make them at home, I wonder why I don't make them weekly. This Paleo-friendly tart is the perfect meal to make ahead of time and to nosh on throughout the week. You can eat it warm or cold and for breakfast, lunch or dinner!

SERVES 8

FOR THE PASTRY CRUST

2 cups (224 g) superfine almond flour

2 cups (256 g) tapioca flour

2 tsp (2 g) chopped fresh rosemary

½ tsp salt

2 tbsp (18 g) coconut sugar

¾ cup (170 g) cold ghee, cut into ½-inch (12-mm) pieces

2 eggs

2 tbsp (30 ml) water

1½ tbsp (23 ml) oil of preference, for greasing

FOR THE FILLING

10 eggs, whisked

2 (3-oz [85-g]) chicken and apple sausages, diced

2 cups (182 g) chopped broccoli

½ yellow onion, diced

1 tsp garlic powder

1½ tsp (9 g) sea salt

1 tsp ground black pepper

For the pastry crust, in a food processor or with a handheld mixer, combine the almond flour, tapioca flour, rosemary, salt and sugar. Add the ghee and pulse or mix again until the ghee is about the size of peas. Add the eggs and water and mix until dough forms. Refrigerate the dough for at least 30 minutes, or up to overnight.

When you are ready to prepare the tart, grease a quarter sheet pan and preheat the oven to 375°F (190°C). On a lightly floured work surface, roll out your dough with a rolling pin into a 10 x 14–inch (25 x 36–cm) rectangle. Arrange the dough on the prepared baking sheet, being sure some of the dough goes up the sides of the pan to form the tart. Poke the dough all over with a fork, and bake it for 10 minutes.

Prepare the filling while the crust is par-baking. To the bowl of eggs, add the sausages, broccoli, onion, garlic powder, salt and pepper. Stir to combine.

When the crust is par-baked, remove it from the oven. Carefully pour the egg mixture over the crust. Bake the tart for 15 minutes, or until the eggs are set.

> **NOTE:** "Par-baking" is partially cooking the dough. This ensures the dough will cook all the way through after adding the filling. It would be a soggy mess if you didn't par-bake.

PROSCIUTTO-WRAPPED ASPARAGUS WITH EGG

I love asparagus! It's one of my favorites. It's fairly easy to roast and a nice, light vegetable to eat in the morning. Add the eggs and you have the Paleo breakfast that will help fuel your body until your next meal. I include the ranch dressing recipe here because it can so easily be made at home, but there are a few great options in grocery stores for Paleo-friendly ranch that you could use instead to save a bit of time.

SERVES 6

FOR THE ASPARAGUS

1 lb (454 g) asparagus, divided

6 slices prosciutto

Avocado oil

6 eggs

FOR THE RANCH DRESSING

1 cup (235 g) Paleo mayonnaise

½ cup (120 ml) unsweetened full-fat coconut milk

1½ tbsp (23 ml) red wine vinegar

½ tsp salt

½ tsp ground black pepper

1 tsp onion powder

1 tsp garlic powder

2 tsp (2 g) dried dill

1 tbsp (2 g) dried parsley

For the asparagus, preheat the oven to 400°F (204°C). Bunch 3 to 4 of the asparagus spears together and wrap them with a piece of prosciutto. Repeat with the remaining asparagus and prosciutto until you have 6 bunches. Arrange the bunches on a large baking sheet so that none of the bunches touch each other. Drizzle a bit of avocado oil over the top of each bunch. Bake the bunches for 5 minutes.

Remove the sheet pan from the oven and carefully crack an egg over the top of each asparagus bunch. Place the pan back in the oven and cook the bunches for another 7 to 10 minutes, or until the eggs are cooked to your liking (an egg cooked over 12 minutes will be hard-boiled).

Prepare the ranch dressing while the asparagus roasts. Mix the mayonnaise, coconut milk and vinegar together in a medium-sized bowl. Stir in the salt, pepper, onion powder, garlic powder, dill and parsley. You can store the ranch dressing in a sealed jar for up to a week in the refrigerator.

Drizzle some of the ranch dressing over the asparagus bunches before serving them.

> **NOTE:** All the mayonnaise in this book is Paleo-approved and delicious. My favorite brands are Primal Kitchen and Tessemae's.

HEAVENLY BLUEBERRY PANCAKES

If you love pancakes then you are really, really going to love these sheet pan blueberry pancakes. First off, they taste so legit, you wouldn't even know that they are Paleo. While it may seem like more effort to use a couple of flours, I promise you the end result is worth it. Also, after making pancakes on a sheet pan, you will never go back to the round version prepared on the stovetop or griddle. This method means you don't have to flip the pancakes, and it makes for super easy cleanup.

SERVES 12

1⅓ cups (170 g) tapioca flour

3 cups (336 g) superfine almond flour

2 tsp (9 g) baking soda

1 tsp sea salt

6 eggs

1 cup (240 ml) unsweetened almond milk

¼ cup (60 ml) honey

1 tbsp plus 1 tsp (20 ml) apple cider vinegar

1 tbsp plus 1 tsp (20 ml) vanilla extract

2 cups (300 g) fresh blueberries

Maple syrup

Ghee, optional

Preheat the oven to 425°F (218°C). Line a sheet pan with parchment paper.

In a large bowl, mix together the tapioca flour, almond flour, baking soda and salt. Add the eggs, almond milk, honey, vinegar and vanilla. Whisk until well combined. Fold the blueberries into the batter, then pour it evenly onto the prepared pan.

Bake the pancake for 8 minutes, or until a toothpick inserted into the center comes out clean.

Cut the pancake into serving-sized pieces and serve them with the maple syrup and dollops of ghee, if using.

TOMATO-BASIL-BACON FRITTATA

Breakfast is the most important meal of the day, and now the most delicious thanks to this Paleo tomato-basil-bacon bake! Whether you are prepping breakfast for the week or hosting a little weekend brunch, you can never go wrong with an egg bake. This flavor combo is amazingly delicious. You can omit the bacon for a delicious vegetarian Paleo version.

SERVES 8

12 eggs, whisked

3 slices sugar-free bacon, chopped

1 cup (139 g) quartered cherry tomatoes

6 fresh basil leaves, chiffonade

1 tsp garlic powder

½ tsp sea salt

Balsamic vinegar

Preheat the oven to 375°F (190°C), and line a baking sheet with parchment paper.

To the bowl of eggs, add the bacon, tomatoes, basil, garlic powder and salt. Stir until the mixture is combined, then pour it over the parchment paper. Bake the frittata for 15 minutes, or until the eggs are set and no longer runny. Drizzle the balsamic vinegar over the top.

Cut the frittata into squares; it can be served hot or cold. The squares will keep in an airtight container in the refrigerator for up to 5 days or in the freezer for up to 3 months. If you freeze the squares, place a piece of wax paper between each one.

RICH AND SAVORY SAUSAGE PATTIES

Sausage patties or links . . . I love them both. But when making things at home, there is no question that the patty is way easier. So, let's make some patties, shall we?

It's hard to find Paleo sausage in grocery stores. Most sausage is filled with junk. When you make sausage at home, you know exactly what is going into them. And that's a big huge huzzah in my book! I also love making sausage patties in the oven, because you can make a bunch and you don't have to worry about getting the sides of your stove greasy. I enjoy these with Pumpkin Spice Pancakes (page 10) or Shakshuka (page 33). Sometimes, if I'm feeling extra fancy, I'll drizzle a bit of maple syrup over the tops of the patties.

MAKES 12 PATTIES

1½ tbsp (23 ml) oil of preference, for greasing

1 lb (454 g) ground pork

½ lb (226 g) ground beef

1 tbsp (2 g) chopped fresh sage

1 tbsp (1 g) chopped fresh thyme

½ tsp fennel seeds

¼ tsp ground allspice

2 cloves garlic, minced

1½ tsp (9 g) sea salt

Preheat the oven to 375°F (190°C) and grease a sheet pan.

Put the pork, beef, sage, thyme, fennel, allspice, garlic and salt in a large bowl. Mix the ingredients with your hands until they are well-combined. Divide the mixture into 12 portions. Shape each portion into a ball, then press it down in your palm to flatten it. To prevent the patties from turning puck-like when they are cooked, press your finger down to make a little dent in the center of the patty. This will make the whole patty cook evenly and not shrink.

Arrange the patties on the prepared pan, and bake them for 20 minutes, or until they are deep golden brown.

GIANT CINNAMON POP-TART

Because this is made from wholesome ingredients and has plenty of good fats, there is no guilt from eating this. Bet you'd never thought anyone would say that about a pop-tart!

SERVES 8

FOR THE PASTRY CRUST

2 cups (224 g) superfine almond flour

2 cups (256 g) tapioca flour

½ tsp salt

2 tbsp (18 g) coconut sugar

¾ cup (170 g) cold ghee, cut into ½-inch (12-mm) pieces

2 eggs

2 tbsp (30 ml) water

FOR THE FILLING

1 cup (144 g) brown coconut sugar

2 tbsp (16 g) ground cinnamon

3 tbsp (24 g) tapioca flour

3 tbsp (45 ml) melted ghee

2 tbsp (30 ml) maple syrup

FOR THE CINNAMON GLAZE

¼ cup (36 g) coconut sugar

½ cup (64 g) tapioca flour

1 tsp ground cinnamon

2 tbsp (30 ml) unsweetened almond milk

For the pastry crust, in a food processor or with a handheld mixer, combine the almond flour, tapioca flour, salt and sugar. Add the ghee, and pulse or mix again until the ghee is about the size of peas. Add the eggs and water and mix until a dough forms. Refrigerate the dough for at least 30 minutes, or up to overnight.

When you are ready to make the pop-tart, preheat the oven to 350°F (177°C), and line a quarter sheet pan with parchment paper.

For the filling, place the sugar, cinnamon, tapioca flour, ghee and maple syrup in a medium-sized bowl. Beat with a handheld mixer until it forms a paste.

With a rolling pin, roll the dough into 2 rectangles, each a little bit smaller than the sheet pan and about ¼ inch (6 mm) thick. Place one rectangle on the prepared sheet pan and spread the filling out, leaving a ½-inch (12-mm) border around the edges. Lay the other piece of dough on top of the filling, and crimp the edges with a fork.

Bake the tart for 25 minutes, or until it is golden brown.

Prepare the cinnamon glaze while the tart is cooling. Whisk the sugar, tapioca flour, cinnamon and almond milk for 30 seconds, or until no clumps remain and the glaze is smooth. Pour the glaze over the tart and let it harden—it takes about 5 minutes—before serving the tart. You can eat the pop-tart while it's still warm or let it cool completely.

SPINACH-CHORIZO EGG BAKE

I really love making egg bakes on a sheet pan. I'm all about variety, and this Spinach-Chorizo Egg Bake gives my family and me exactly that! Chorizo is a very flavorful meat and one of my favorites to pair with eggs. Not only is this recipe perfect for weekday mornings, it is also fantastic for get-togethers and weekend brunches.

SERVES 8

1½ tbsp (23 ml) oil of preference, for greasing

12 eggs, whisked

1 (4-oz [113-g]) jar diced pimientos, drained

1 (11-oz [312-g]) package chorizo sausage, diced (We like the Silva brand.)

½ red onion, diced

1 cup (30 g) packed chopped spinach

2 tsp (12 g) sea salt

1 tsp garlic powder

Salsa, optional

Sliced avocado, optional

Preheat the oven to 375°F (190°C). Grease a quarter sheet pan with some ghee or oil.

To the bowl of eggs, add the pimientos, chorizo, onion, spinach, salt and garlic powder. Gently stir to combine, and then pour the mixture into the prepared pan.

Carefully place the sheet pan into the oven, and cook the egg bake for 15 minutes, or until the eggs are set and no longer runny. Cut the egg bake into squares, and garnish the squares with the salsa and avocado, if using.

PERFECTLY BAKED BREAKFAST TAQUITOS

My family is very lucky to live in a culturally diverse area in California, where we experience a lot of unbelievable cuisines. I have to say that Mexican food is the best out here! Taquitos are usually eaten at dinner, but I decided to make them as a hearty, energy-fueling Paleo breakfast with kale and eggs.

SERVES 8

FOR THE CASHEW CHEESE

1 cup (134 g) raw cashews

2 tbsp (10 g) nutritional yeast

2 cloves garlic, minced

½ tsp sea salt dissolved in ¼ cup (60 ml) water

Juice of ½ lemon

FOR THE TAQUITOS

1½ tbsp (23 ml) oil of preference, for greasing

2 cups (134 g) baby kale

8 eggs, whisked

½ lb (226 g) ground pork, raw

½ lb (226 g) ground beef, raw

2 tsp (5 g) chili powder

1 tsp dried oregano

1 tsp ground cumin

12 Paleo-friendly tortillas, divided

Avocado oil spray

Pico de gallo

Fresh cilantro sprigs, optional

For the cashew cheese, place the cashews in a bowl, and cover them with water to soak for at least 1 hour. Drain the soaking water from the cashews. In a blender, blend the cashews, nutritional yeast, garlic, salt water and lemon juice for 30 seconds, or until the mixture is smooth and creamy.

For the taquitos, preheat the oven to 375°F (190°C), and grease a quarter sheet pan. Grease a skillet. Fold the kale into the bowl of eggs, then pour the egg mixture into the skillet. Cook, stirring, over medium-low heat, until the eggs are scrambled, about 2½ minutes. Transfer the eggs to a large mixing bowl, then add the pork, beef, chili powder, oregano and cumin. Mix to combine.

Scoop ½ cup (112 g) of the meat and egg mixture into the middle of a tortilla, then spoon about 2 tablespoons (30 g) of the cashew cheese over the egg mixture. Roll up the tortilla and place it, seam-side down, onto the prepared baking sheet. Repeat the process to make 8 taquitos, arranged in a single layer on the baking sheet.

Spray the tops of the taquitos with the avocado oil. Bake them for 20 minutes, or until they are crispy and golden brown. Top with some of the pico de gallo and drizzle a little more of the cashew cheese over the top. Garnish with the cilantro, if using.

> **NOTES:** If you don't use all of the cashew cheese for this recipe, store the remaining cheese in an airtight container in the refrigerator for up to 1 week.
>
> I like to chop up some veggies and use this cheese as dip. You can also use it for the Jalapeño-Popper Stuffed Chicken (page 42) as well!

FLUFFY PALEO EGG CLOUDS

These are a fun Paleo breakfast to have when you want to feel oh-so-classy. Fluffy Paleo Egg Clouds look super gourmet but are actually very, very simple to make, and they will win the hearts of anyone eating them! The clouds are best served right out of the oven, so make sure everyone is at the table with their fork and knife in hand when the clouds are ready.

SERVES 6

6 eggs, whites separated from yolks

1 tsp sea salt

½ tsp ground black pepper

¼ cup (57 g) crumbled cooked sugar-free bacon

1 tbsp (3 g) chopped fresh chives

Paleo-friendly hot sauce, optional

Preheat the oven to 450°F (232°C). Line your baking sheet with parchment paper.

With a mixer, beat the egg whites for about 5 to 8 minutes, or until stiff peaks form. Stiff peaks are formed when you lift the beater and you get a peak that holds its shape. Divide the egg whites into 6 mounds on the prepared pan, then make deep wells in the center of each mound with the back of a tablespoon.

Bake the egg whites for 3 minutes. Remove the pan from the oven and put one yolk into each of the wells. Put the sheet pan back into the oven and cook the clouds for another 3 minutes, or until the egg whites are light golden brown.

Top the clouds with the salt, pepper, bacon, chives and hot sauce, if using. Serve immediately.

NOTE: To separate egg whites from the yolks, over a mixing bowl, crack an egg into your hand. Move the egg carefully between your hands, letting the whites fall off between your fingers and into the mixing bowl. Place the yolks on a plate until you are ready to put them into the egg clouds.

SHAKSHUKA

Shakshuka is a satisfying and hearty sheet pan meal and is nothing short of heavenly! You literally pour everything onto the sheet pan and let your oven do its thing. This is packed full of protein, and the tomatoes are rich in vitamins, making this the perfect dish to start your morning. A handful of arugula goes really well alongside this meal.

SERVES 6

2 ancho chiles, seeded and diced

1 red bell pepper, diced

2 cloves garlic, minced

2 (28-oz [798-g]) cans fire-roasted diced tomatoes, with liquid

1½ tsp (3 g) ground cumin

1½ tsp (3 g) sweet paprika

1 tsp dried minced onion

1 tsp sea salt

6 eggs

Fresh lime juice

Handful of fresh cilantro

Fresh arugula, microgreens or sliced avocado, optional

Preheat the oven to 375°F (190°C). Spread the ancho chiles, bell pepper and garlic onto a sheet pan. Pour the tomatoes onto the baking sheet. Sprinkle the cumin, paprika, onion and salt all over the tomatoes. Stir the mixture to combine the ingredients, and spread it to fill the entire baking sheet.

Put the sheet pan into the oven and cook the shakshuka for 15 minutes. Carefully remove the sheet pan. Crack 6 eggs on top of the tomatoes, and then return the pan to the oven.

Let the shakshuka bake for another 10 minutes, or until the tomatoes are bubbly and the eggs are set and no longer runny. Garnish the shakshuka with the lime juice and cilantro, then top it with the arugula, if using.

PALEO BREAKFAST BISCUITS

I love a good piece of bread or biscuit alongside my morning breakfast. You can use these biscuits to make breakfast sausage sandwiches using the Rich and Savory Sausage Patties (page 22) or just eat them with honey or jam. If you want to get crazy, save some to eat with soup!

SERVES 10

1½ tbsp (23 ml) oil of preference, for greasing

¼ cup (60 ml) unsweetened almond milk

¼ tsp apple cider vinegar

2¼ cups (252 g) superfine almond flour

1 cup (128 g) tapioca flour, plus more if needed

1½ tsp (6 g) baking powder

1 tsp sea salt

5 tbsp (71 g) cold ghee, cut into ½-tbsp (7-g) pieces

2 eggs

Paleo jam, ghee or honey, optional

Preheat the oven to 400°F (204°C), and lightly grease a sheet pan.

Mix together the almond milk and vinegar, and set aside the mixture. In a food processor (or you can use your hands), mix together the almond flour, tapioca flour, baking powder and salt. Add the ghee, and blend it in until the mixture is the consistency of sand.

Add the milk mixture and eggs and mix until a dough is formed. If the dough is sticky, add tapioca flour, 1 tablespoon (8 g) at a time. Shape the dough into 10 balls the size of your palm. Arrange the balls, 1 inch (2.5 cm) apart, on the prepared pan. Slightly press down on each biscuit with your hand to flatten it.

Bake for 20 minutes, or until the biscuits are golden brown. Serve with the jam, if using.

Main Dishes
FROM OVEN TO PLATE!

I get it. Eating clean can be hard, especially at the end of a long work day. That's why sheet pan meals are the "sheet!" Sheet pan meals make cooking and cleanup a cinch and are a great way to get your family eating delicious, healthy Paleo dishes. I can't wait for you to try the Jalapeño-Popper Stuffed Chicken (page 42) and the Green Chili Pork Chops with Stuffed Poblanos (page 62). The key to a killer sheet pan dinner is mixing it up and trying different flavor combos. Have fun and get creative. Better yet, if you have kids, get them involved as well. Showing them how important it is to eat wholesome meals when they are young will help them stay healthy as they get older.

PEPPERCORN BALSAMIC TRI-TIP

Tri-tip is a fantastic cut of meat from the bottom tip of the sirloin. It gets its name from its triangular shape. This cut of meat is very tender, juicy and lower in fat than other cuts of beef. Grilled or oven roasted, this peppercorn tri-tip flavor is unbeatable. This protein goes well with any and every kind of vegetable and is wonderful over mixed greens for lunches or a light dinner.

SERVES 6–8

2 lbs (907 g) tri-tip steak

¼ cup (60 ml) balsamic vinegar

3 cloves garlic, minced

2 tbsp (13 g) crushed tri-color peppercorns

2 lbs (907 g) broccoli florets

Avocado oil

2 tsp (12 g) sea salt

In a resealable plastic bag or a bowl, place the tri-tip, vinegar and garlic. Shake the bag or stir the mixture to coat the steak. If you've used a bowl, cover it tightly. Marinate the meat in the refrigerator for at least 1 hour, or up to overnight.

When you are ready to cook the meat, preheat the oven to 425° F (218°C), and line a sheet pan with aluminum foil.

Put your tri-tip in the middle of the pan. Rub the peppercorns over the entire tri-tip. Surround the tri-tip with the broccoli florets, drizzle the florets with the oil and sprinkle the tri-tip and the broccoli with the salt.

Cook the meat for 25 minutes, or until its internal temperature reaches 145°F (63°C) on an instant-read thermometer. If the meat still hasn't reached 145°F (63°C), but the broccoli is cooked, remove the broccoli from the pan, cover it with foil to keep it warm and set it aside until the tri-tip is done roasting.

Remove the steak from the oven and lightly cover it with aluminum foil for 10 minutes to let it rest. The meat will continue to cook as it rests. After it rests, slice the tri-tip against the grain and serve it with the broccoli.

CHICKEN TENDERS WITH HONEY CHIPOTLE SAUCE

There are few things that are better than a nice crispy chicken tender. But I love knowing exactly what is going into my food, and the chicken tenders you see at the store are anything but healthy. These chicken tenders are a major upgrade from the usual over-processed, deep-fried junk. If you like things extra spicy, double up the chipotle! These pair really well with the Tandoori Mixed Veggies (page 112) and the Honey-Glazed Brussels Sprouts (page 108).

SERVES 6–8

FOR THE CHICKEN

2 eggs

1 cup (112 g) superfine almond flour

1 tsp sea salt

1½ tsp (3 g) ground turmeric

1 tsp garlic powder

1 tbsp (2 g) dried parsley

2 tbsp (16 g) arrowroot powder

2 lbs (907 g) chicken tenders

FOR THE HONEY CHIPOTLE SAUCE

1 cup (235 g) Paleo mayonnaise
(I like Primal Kitchen or Tessemae's.)

¼ cup (60 ml) honey

1 tbsp (8 g) chipotle powder

1 tsp salt

For the chicken, preheat the oven to 375°F (190°C), and line a sheet pan with parchment paper.

Whisk the eggs in a small, shallow bowl. In another bowl, mix together the almond flour, salt, turmeric, garlic powder, parsley and arrowroot powder. Dredge each piece of chicken by dipping it in the egg, then the flour mixture. Place each piece of chicken on the prepared pan, spacing them evenly apart and not touching each other.

Put the sheet pan in the oven and cook the chicken for 20 to 25 minutes, flipping once, until the breading is golden brown and crispy.

Prepare the honey chipotle sauce while the chicken is baking. In a small bowl, mix the mayonnaise, honey, chipotle powder and salt until the mixture is well-combined. Adjust the sweetness by adding more honey or the heat by adding more chipotle powder.

JALAPEÑO-POPPER STUFFED CHICKEN

If you are newer to the Paleo diet, I highly suggest this stuffed chicken! When my husband took his first bite of this meal, he immediately said that this was on his list of the top three best dishes he has ever had. After he practically ate the entire sheet pan of food, I told him I made the cheese with cashews. He was amazed that something that delicious was completely Paleo. If I'm lucky enough to have leftovers, I like to cut up the chicken and place it over some fresh mixed greens.

SERVES 6

Cashew Cheese (page 29)

½ cup (45 g) chopped jalapeños

2–3 slices chopped sugar-free bacon, divided

6 large chicken breasts

Sea salt

Ground black pepper

1 lb (454 g) green beans

Avocado oil

Preheat the oven to 375°F (190°C).

Mix the cashew cheese, jalapeños and two-thirds of the bacon in a medium-sized bowl.

Cut a pocket into each of the chicken breasts by making a horizontal slice, being careful not to cut all the way through the chicken breast. Stuff one-sixth of the cheese mixture into each chicken pocket. Place the chicken on your sheet pan, and sprinkle the breasts with the salt and pepper. Arrange the green beans between the chicken pieces and sprinkle the remaining one-third of the bacon over the green beans. Drizzle the green beans and chicken with the avocado oil.

Bake the chicken and veggies for 30 to 35 minutes, or until the chicken is golden brown and the internal temperature is 160°F (71°C) on an instant-read thermometer. Every oven is different, so keep an eye on the green beans. Remove them if you see them getting a little toasty!

CHILI-LIME SALMON WITH MANGO RELISH

Salmon is a favorite in our house. My whole family loves it! Salmon is packed full of protein, which is important to have while eating Paleo. Salmon is also rich in omega-3 fatty acids, which promote brain health. Also, come close, I have a secret to tell you: You should put your salmon into a cold oven for the most perfectly cooked fish every time.

SERVES 6

FOR THE SEASONING MIXTURE

1½ tsp (3 g) smoked paprika

1 tsp dried oregano

2 tsp (5 g) chili powder

1 tsp garlic powder

1½ tsp (9 g) sea salt

1 tsp ground cumin

FOR THE SALMON

2 (10-oz [283-g]) bags cauliflower rice

6 wild-caught salmon fillets

2 tbsp (30 ml) avocado oil

Juice of 2 large limes

FOR THE MANGO RELISH

2 avocados, diced

1 large mango, diced

½ red onion, diced

Juice of 1 orange

1 tbsp (15 ml) honey

½ cup (8 g) chopped fresh cilantro

1 tsp sea salt

For the seasoning, in a small bowl, mix together the paprika, oregano, chili powder, garlic powder, salt and cumin.

For the salmon, spread out the cauliflower rice on a sheet pan. Place your salmon fillets on top of the cauliflower rice. If the salmon has skin, place it skin-side down. Rub the avocado oil into the top of the salmon. Generously sprinkle the seasoning mixture all over the salmon and cauliflower rice. Sprinkle the lime juice over the salmon.

Place a rack in the middle of your oven, and put the baking sheet with the salmon on the rack. Now, turn on the oven to 400°F (204°C), and set the timer for 25 minutes.

Prepare the mango relish while the salmon is cooking. In a small bowl, mix the avocados, mango, onion, orange juice and honey. Add the cilantro and salt and mix until combined.

Remove the salmon when the 25 minutes is up or when the fish flakes easily with a fork. For serving, top the fillets with the mango relish.

MEDITERRANEAN PIZZA

I don't think I've ever met anyone who doesn't like pizza. There is a pizza joint in Berkeley, California, that has the best ever Mediterranean pizza, which usually consists of briny olives and artichoke hearts, tomatoes and tons of cheese! That is until now. This sheet pan Paleo pizza is so unbelievable, you won't know or even care that there isn't any cheese or gluten.

SERVES 8

1½ tbsp (23 ml) avocado oil, for greasing

FOR THE DOUGH

1 cup (112 g) superfine almond flour

1½ cups (168 g) cassava flour

¾ cup (96 g) tapioca flour, plus more if needed

1 tsp garlic powder

1 tsp dried rosemary

1½ cups (360 ml) warm water

⅔ cup (160 ml) avocado oil, plus more for drizzling

2 tbsp (30 ml) apple cider vinegar

2 eggs, whisked

FOR THE TOPPINGS

3 cloves garlic, finely chopped

Handful of spinach

1 (15-oz [425-g]) jar roasted red peppers, drained and sliced

1 cup (180 g) Kalamata olives

½ red onion, thinly sliced

1 (14-oz [397-g]) can water-packed quartered artichoke hearts, drained

Shredded cooked chicken, optional

Preheat the oven to 450°F (232°C). Grease a quarter sheet pan with some oil.

To make the dough, mix the almond flour, cassava flour, tapioca flour, garlic powder and rosemary together. Next, stir the water, oil and vinegar into the flour mixture. Pour your eggs into the flour mixture, and mix until a dough has formed. If it is a bit too sticky, add a little more tapioca flour, 1 tablespoon (8 g) at a time.

After the dough is made, spread it out and press it onto the prepared baking sheet. You want it pretty thin—no more than ½ inch (12 mm)—to make sure the dough cooks all the way through. Once your dough is all spread out, poke holes in it with a fork, and drizzle some avocado oil over the top. Bake the dough for 10 minutes.

For the toppings, spread the garlic and spinach over the par-baked dough. Then add the peppers, olives, onion and artichoke hearts. If you are using chicken, add that to the top. Drizzle with a bit more oil and bake for another 10 minutes, or until the toppings are warmed through.

Carefully remove the pizza from the oven, let it cool for 5 minutes and slice it into squares.

CRISPY BEEF AND BROCCOLI

Beef and broccoli is one of my absolute favorite dishes to order when I go out for Chinese food. But I never feel great after eating it, and I'm sure a lot of you feel the same. This recipe was created so that you can still enjoy the deliciousness of take-out with no regrets! I love how full of flavor this dish is while still keeping it simple. Feel free to add more vegetables if you'd like. I like to serve this with the "Fried" Cauliflower Rice (page 96).

SERVES 4–6

2 lbs (907 g) sirloin steak, cut against the grain into ½-inch (12-mm) slices

1 tsp dried minced onion

1 tsp garlic powder

½ tsp sea salt

1 tbsp (15 ml) rice vinegar

½ cup (120 ml) coconut aminos

2 tbsp (32 g) tomato paste

1 lb (454 g) broccoli florets

3 tbsp (24 g) arrowroot powder

Sliced green onions, optional

In a large bowl, place the steak, onion, garlic powder, salt, vinegar, coconut aminos and tomato paste. Toss to combine.

Next, add the broccoli and the arrowroot powder to the bowl. Toss again to combine everything. Cover the bowl, and let the mixture marinate in the refrigerator for at least 1 hour, or up to overnight.

When you are ready to cook the beef and broccoli, preheat the oven to 450°F (232°C), and line a sheet pan with parchment paper. Pour the bowl of steak and broccoli onto the pan and evenly spread out the ingredients.

Cook the beef and broccoli for 12 minutes, or until the broccoli can be easily pierced with a fork and its ends are brown and the beef looks crispy. Sprinkle the green onions over the pan, if you are using them.

FAJITA MEATBALLS WITH SQUASH AND CILANTRO-LIME DRESSING

Oven-roasted meatballs are always a huge hit in our house. The flavors of fajita meatballs and squash are a match made in heaven. If you aren't typically a fan of squash, try delicata . . . you will start seeing it in stores early fall through winter. Stock up, because this will easily become your favorite vegetable.

SERVES 6

FOR THE FAJITA SEASONING

2 tsp (5 g) chili powder

2 tsp (12 g) sea salt

1 tbsp (7 g) sweet paprika

1½ tsp (4 g) onion powder

1½ tsp (4 g) garlic powder

1 tsp ground cumin

1½ tsp (3 g) dried oregano

¼ tsp cayenne pepper

FOR THE MEATBALLS

2 lbs (907 g) ground beef

1 egg

2 delicata squash, seeded and sliced

1½ tbsp (23 ml) olive oil

Fresh cilantro sprigs, for serving

FOR THE CILANTRO-LIME DRESSING

¼ cup (56 g) Paleo mayonnaise
(I like Primal Kitchen or Tessemae's.)

1 cup (16 g) cilantro, packed

1 large clove garlic, minced

2 tbsp (30 ml) red wine vinegar

3 tbsp (45 ml) avocado oil

Juice of ½ lime

Pinch of salt

Preheat the oven to 375°F (190°C). Place a wire rack over your baking sheet so the meatballs don't sit in their juices. If you don't have a wire rack, line the pan with parchment paper.

For the fajita seasoning, in a medium-sized bowl, mix the chili powder, salt, paprika, onion powder, garlic powder, cumin, oregano and cayenne. Transfer 1½ tablespoons (7 g) of the seasoning into a large bowl.

For the meatballs, add the beef and egg to the bowl with the 1½ tablespoons (7 g) of the fajita seasoning, and mix together well, using your hands. Roll pieces of the mixture into 1½-inch (4-cm) balls.

Place your meatballs on the wire rack. Place the squash in a bowl, and drizzle it with a little oil. Add the remaining fajita seasoning and toss to coat. Arrange the squash around the meatballs on the wire rack. Cook the meatballs and squash in the oven for 20 minutes, or until the squash is golden brown and slightly crispy and the meatballs have browned.

Prepare the dressing while the meatballs and squash cook. In a blender or food processor, mix the mayonnaise, cilantro, garlic, vinegar, avocado oil, lime juice and salt until smooth, about 30 to 45 seconds.

For serving, spread as much of the dressing as you like over the meatballs and squash, and garnish the plates with the cilantro sprigs.

> NOTE: The Cilantro-Lime Dressing is spectacular on anything and everything; it will last in the fridge for a week in an airtight container.

STEAK-WRAPPED PEPPER ROLLS

This weeknight meal is sure to win the hearts of your entire family. This cut of meat cooks up quickly, making it the perfect ingredient for those busy nights when you really don't want to cook but do want to put a healthy, balanced meal on the table! Using three different colors of peppers appeals to the eye and pairs perfectly with the steak and balsamic vinegar. Your mouth will thank you after taking a bite of these. This recipe pairs well with the Buffalo Roasted Cauliflower (page 87).

SERVES 6

2 lbs (907 g) flank steak, cut into 2-inch (5-cm) slices

1 tsp dried oregano

1 tsp dried rosemary

1½ tsp (9 g) sea salt

½ tsp ground black pepper

¼ cup (60 ml) balsamic vinegar, plus more to drizzle

3 large tri-colored bell peppers, sliced

Preheat the oven to 425°F (218°C).

Place the steak in a large mixing bowl, and add the oregano, rosemary, salt, pepper and balsamic vinegar. Toss to coat the meat.

Lay a slice of beef on a work surface. Place a few slices of the bell peppers on the middle of the steak. Roll up the steak and put it, seam-side down, onto a sheet pan. Repeat with the remaining slices of steak and bell peppers, arranging the rolls so that they do not touch each other.

Cook the rolls for 7 to 9 minutes, or until the internal temperature of the beef reaches 130°F (54°C) on an instant-read thermometer. Drizzle a little more balsamic over the top of each roll once they've finished cooking.

PESTO CHICKEN WITH CAULIFLOWER

This sheet pan dinner is a family favorite and yours will go nuts over it! Seriously, my kids ask for this weekly. I often double the recipe because it makes great leftovers for lunch or even breakfast. Yes, that's right, breakfast. Mix leftovers with some eggs to make a delicious Paleo scramble. We also enjoy tossing it with some mixed greens for a simple and flavorful salad.

SERVES 6

FOR THE CHICKEN

2 lbs (907 g) cauliflower florets

Avocado oil

1½ tsp (9 g) sea salt

12 oz (340 g) cherry tomatoes

1 (14.5-oz [411-g]) can sliced black olives, drained

1 (14-oz [397-g]) can water-packed quartered artichoke hearts, drained

6 chicken breasts

Fresh basil leaves

FOR THE PESTO

3 cups (72 g) packed fresh basil leaves

2 cloves garlic, minced

Juice of ½ lemon

½ cup (120 ml) extra virgin olive oil

Pinch of salt

¼ cup (32 g) pine nuts, optional

For the chicken, preheat the oven to 375°F (190°C). Place the cauliflower florets on your sheet pan, drizzle them with the oil, sprinkle the salt on them and toss until they are coated. Put the cauliflower into the oven and let it cook for 10 minutes.

Prepare the pesto while the cauliflower is cooking. In a blender, blend the basil, garlic, lemon juice, oil, salt and pine nuts, if using, until the mixture is smooth.

To continue preparing the chicken, remove the cauliflower from the oven after 10 minutes of cooking. Add the tomatoes, olives and artichoke hearts to the cauliflower and toss together the vegetables with half of the pesto sauce. Arrange the chicken over the cauliflower, drizzle the chicken with avocado oil and spoon the rest of the pesto over the chicken breasts. Reduce the oven temperature to 350°F (177°C). Return the sheet pan to the oven and cook the meal for another 25 to 30 minutes, or until the chicken is no longer pink.

For serving, garnish with the basil.

How fancy does this meal sound?! It really is quite simple. *En papillote* simply means that the fish is cooked in a packet, in this case parchment. This is a foolproof way of making a tender, flaky, flavorful fish. Use any fresh seasonal veggies that sound good to you!

SERVES 4

4 wild-caught salmon fillets

½ shallot, diced

¾ cup (12 g) chopped fresh cilantro

3 cloves garlic, minced

1 cup (240 ml) balsamic vinegar

1 large sweet potato, cut into 1¼-inch (3-cm) slices

1¼ tsp (7 g) sea salt

1 tsp ground black pepper

12 green onions, sliced into thirds

Put the salmon in a resealable plastic bag. Mix the shallot, cilantro, garlic and balsamic vinegar in a small bowl, then pour the mixture over the salmon. Let the salmon marinate in the refrigerator for 1 hour.

Preheat the oven to 425°F (218°C). Rip 4 pieces of parchment paper for the fish—the size depends on the size of your fillets, but 10 to 12 inches (25 to 30.5 cm) wide usually works.

Divide the sweet potato slices among the pieces of parchment paper. Put a marinated salmon fillet on top of each of the sweet potato stacks, then sprinkle the salt and pepper over the salmon. Top each salmon fillet with one-quarter of the green onions.

Working with one packet at a time, pull the long sides of the parchment up to meet above the fish, then fold one side of the paper over the other. Roll the folded edges down toward the fish. Next, press the short ends of the parchment together toward each other, then fold them in to seal the packets. The seal need not be tight. Lay the packets on your sheet pan and bake them for 15 minutes.

Remove the packets from the oven and let them rest for a few minutes, or until the paper is cool enough for you to unfold the packets. Be careful, as steam will billow out of the packet once it gets opened. You can plate the fish or eat it straight from the packet for even easier cleanup.

SPAGHETTI SQUASH PORK CHOW MEIN

If I did a poll right now, I bet 99 percent of you would say that you get chow mein every time you go to an Asian restaurant. If I took another poll, I'm sure 99 percent of you would say you feel terrible afterward; I know I always do! This chow mein will never make you feel sick after, because it uses the freshest of produce. If you do not eat pork, you may substitute chicken or just leave out meat for a vegetarian version.

SERVES 6-8

1 large spaghetti squash, cut in half horizontally and seeded

1 lb (454 g) thin pork chops, sliced

2 carrots, finely diced

1 shallot, chopped

2 cloves garlic, minced

1 rib celery, finely diced

2 cups (140 g) shredded cabbage

2 tsp (5 g) arrowroot powder

¼ cup (60 ml) coconut aminos

1 tsp fish sauce

2 green onions, sliced

Preheat the oven to 400°F (204°C). Place the squash, cut-side down, onto a sheet pan. Bake it for 35 minutes.

In a small bowl, combine the pork, carrots, shallot, garlic, celery, cabbage, arrowroot, coconut aminos and the fish sauce.

Once 35 minutes is up, carefully remove the squash from the oven, and allow it to cool until you can handle it. Scoop out the squash strands with a fork, then place them on the sheet pan you used to roast the squash. Evenly spread the squash. Spread the pork and vegetable mixture over the top of the spaghetti squash. Return the pan to the oven and cook for another 15 minutes, or until the vegetables are fork tender and the pork is golden brown.

Toss together the pork, vegetables and squash. Garnish the chow mein with the green onions.

BUTTERMILK-DRENCHED CAVEMAN POPS

Turkey legs, or in the Paleo world, caveman pops, are a fun dish and a nice change from eating chicken. I like the legs because they have the dark meat, which is the best in my opinion. Make sure you save the bones to make homemade bone broth.

SERVES 3

FOR THE BUTTERMILK

2 (13.5-oz [398-ml]) cans unsweetened full-fat coconut milk

3 tbsp (45 ml) apple cider vinegar

2 tbsp (6 g) dried dill

FOR THE TURKEY

3 large turkey legs

2 large sweet potatoes, diced

Avocado oil spray

2 tbsp (6 g) dried dill

2 tbsp (17 g) garlic powder

2 tsp (12 g) sea salt

Fresh thyme sprigs

To make the buttermilk, mix together the coconut milk and the vinegar. Let the mixture sit for 10 minutes. Mix the dill into the buttermilk.

For the turkey, put the legs in a large bowl or dish, and pour half of the buttermilk over them, making sure to coat them well. Let them marinate in the refrigerator for at least 30 minutes, or up to overnight. Refrigerate the remaining buttermilk.

When you are ready to cook the turkey, preheat the oven to 425°F (218°C). Arrange the turkey legs on a sheet pan and cook them in the oven for 10 minutes.

Remove the turkey legs from the oven and flip them over, using tongs. Add the sweet potatoes to the sheet pan, spray oil over the potatoes and sprinkle them with the dill and garlic powder. Return the pan to the oven and cook the turkey and potatoes for another 10 minutes.

Once the time is up, rotate the turkey legs one more time and toss the sweet potatoes. Pour the remaining buttermilk onto the turkey legs. Put them back in the oven and roast them for 10 more minutes, or until the thickest part of the meat registers 155°F (68°C) on an instant-read thermometer. Take the turkey and sweet potatoes out of the oven, and let the turkey rest for 10 minutes, or until the internal temperature reaches 165°F (74°C) on an instant-read thermometer. Sprinkle the turkey and potatoes with the salt and garnish them with the thyme.

GREEN CHILI PORK CHOPS WITH STUFFED POBLANOS

These pork chops will soon be on your weekly menu. They are simple, high in protein and oh-so-scrumptious. Despite what you might have heard about pork, it is very easy to cook. I prefer thick-cut pork chops, because they are more tender and don't dry out as easily as thin-cut chops. A meat thermometer works wonders for cooking perfect pork, so go get one!

SERVES 6

FOR THE PORK

6 pork chops

3 (4-oz [113-g]) cans diced green chiles, drained

½ red onion, diced

1 tsp ground cumin

1½ tsp (3 g) smoked paprika

1½ tsp (3 g) dried oregano

2 tsp (12 g) sea salt

FOR THE STUFFED POBLANOS

3 poblanos, seeded and halved lengthwise

1 (10-oz [283-g]) bag cauliflower rice

2 tbsp (2 g) dried cilantro

½ tsp sea salt

Cashew Cheese (page 29)

For the pork, preheat the oven to 425°F (218°C), and line a sheet pan with parchment paper.

Place the pork chops on your baking sheet, leaving space between them for the poblanos. In a small bowl, mix together the chiles, onion, cumin, paprika, oregano and salt. Spread one-sixth of the green chile mixture on each pork chop.

Arrange the poblanos, cut-side up, between the pork chops. Mix together the cauliflower rice, cilantro, salt and cashew cheese. Stuff one-sixth of the mixture into each poblano.

Reduce the oven temperature to 350°F (177°C), and put the sheet pan in the oven. Cook the pork for 35 minutes, or until the internal temperature of the meat reaches 150°F (65°C) on an instant-read thermometer. Remove the pan from the oven, cover the chops loosely with foil and let them rest for 5 minutes.

BANH MI CHICKEN MEATBALLS

When you hear the word meatball, what do you think of first? Italian food, right? Sure, an Italian meatball is to die for, but have you ever had a Paleo banh mi meatball? Also to die for. Want to know what makes these meatballs amazing . . . it's the radish. Radishes are so often forgotten, mostly because people don't know what to do with them. They are readily available year-round and give the dish a slight peppery flavor. I'm so excited for you to enjoy your new favorite meatball.

SERVES 6

3 lbs (1.4 kg) ground chicken

¼ cup (60 ml) coconut aminos

1 tbsp (15 ml) fish sauce

2 cloves garlic, minced

2 tbsp (28 g) Paleo mayonnaise (I like Primal Kitchen or Tessemae's.)

¼ cup (50 g) finely chopped radish

¼ cup (60 ml) sugar-free Sriracha, plus more for garnish

3 zucchini squash, sliced

¼ cup (75 g) sugar-free pickled veggies or kimchi

Chopped fresh cilantro, optional

Preheat the oven to 375°F (190°C), and place a wire rack on a sheet pan (line the pan with parchment paper if you don't have a wire rack).

In a medium-sized bowl, mix the chicken, coconut aminos, fish sauce, garlic, mayonnaise, radish and Sriracha until it's well-blended.

Form 2-inch (5-cm) meatballs by rolling the meat in the palm of your hand. Arrange the meatballs on the rack in the prepared pan, then place the zucchini slices around the meatballs.

Cook the meatballs and zucchini for 15 minutes, or until they are golden brown. Garnish the dish with the Sriracha and pickled veggies and the cilantro, if using.

CAJUN SHRIMP AND VEGGIES WITH SPICY SLAW

This is a great Paleo weeknight meal. It's quick and easy to prepare and the flavor profile is out-of-this-world good! It has some zing to it, which we absolutely adore in our house. Feel free to cut a bit of the cayenne pepper if you are worried about it being too spicy! You can always add more later. Warning: I have a hard time not eating half of this dish before serving it, so make a lot, because it will go fast.

SERVES 4–6

FOR THE CREOLE SEASONING

2 tbsp (9 g) smoked paprika

1 tbsp (7 g) dried oregano

2 tsp (6 g) garlic powder

1 tsp sea salt

½ tsp cayenne pepper

FOR THE SHRIMP AND VEGGIES

1 large sweet potato, diced

2 red bell peppers, sliced

½ yellow onion, diced

1½ tbsp (23 ml) avocado oil

2 tbsp (9 g) plus 1 tsp Creole Seasoning, divided

1½ lbs (680 g) raw medium shrimp, peeled and deveined

Paleo-friendly hot sauce, optional

Fresh parsley sprigs, optional

FOR THE SPICY SLAW

3 cups (210 g) shredded cabbage

½ cup (119 g) Paleo mayonnaise (I like Primal Kitchen or Tessemae's.)

1 tsp Creole Seasoning

½ tsp Paleo-friendly hot sauce

For the Creole seasoning, in a small bowl, combine the paprika, oregano, garlic powder, salt and cayenne.

For the shrimp and veggies, preheat the oven to 400°F (204°C), and line a baking sheet with parchment paper. Place the sweet potato, bell peppers and onion on the prepared pan, then toss them with the oil and 1 teaspoon of the Creole seasoning. Arrange the vegetables in a single layer, then bake them for 20 minutes.

Prepare the spicy slaw while the vegetables are cooking. In a medium-sized bowl, mix together the cabbage, mayonnaise, Creole seasoning and hot sauce. You can make the slaw spicier by adding more hot sauce. Cover the bowl, and refrigerate the slaw.

Put the shrimp in a bowl and toss it with 2 tablespoons (9 g) of Creole seasoning. After the vegetables have cooked for 20 minutes, remove the sheet pan and spread the shrimp over the vegetables. Return the pan to the oven and cook the shrimp and veggies for another 7 to 10 minutes, or until the shrimp are pink and opaque.

For serving, arrange the shrimp and vegetables on top of the slaw. Garnish the dish with the hot sauce and the parsley, if using.

NOTES: You will not use all of the Creole seasoning mix for this recipe; store the remaining seasoning in a sealed glass jar with your spices for up to 3 months.

Cholula, Tabasco and Frank's RedHot are all great Paleo-friendly hot sauce options!

PALEO LOMO SALTADO (PERUVIAN-STIR FRY)

This is my husband's favorite meal that I make. Lomo saltado is so vibrantly flavorful that it's no wonder he asks for this weekly. This dish mixes the flavors of Peru into a Chinese stir-fry, making it uniquely delicious and a definite must-cook! I like to serve this with a side of the Roasted Brussels Sprouts with Bacon and Chili Vinaigrette (page 99).

SERVES 8

2 lbs (907 g) skirt steak, sliced

1 red onion, thinly sliced

2 red bell peppers, sliced

1 tbsp (15 ml) melted ghee

2 tbsp (30 ml) coconut aminos

3 tbsp (45 ml) red wine vinegar

2 tsp (4 g) ground cumin

1½ tbsp (21 g) ghee or oil of preference, for greasing

2 heaping cups (278 g) cherry tomatoes

2 green onions, cut into 1-inch (2.5-cm) slices

Pickled jalapeños, optional

Put the steak, onion and bell peppers in a resealable plastic bag. Add the ghee, coconut aminos, vinegar and cumin; shake the bag to coat everything with the marinade. Marinate the meat and vegetables in the refrigerator for at least 1 hour, or up to 6 hours.

When you are ready to make the lomo saltado, preheat the oven to 425°F (218°C), and grease a sheet pan with ghee or oil. Arrange the marinated steak and vegetables on the prepared pan, then add the tomatoes and green onions.

Bake the lomo saltado for 7 minutes. Remove the pan from the oven and stir all of the ingredients. Return the pan to the oven and cook the lomo saltado for another 7 minutes, or until the bell peppers can be easily pierced with a fork and the tomatoes are soft.

For serving, garnish the lomo saltado with the pickled jalapeños, if using.

KOREAN BEEF TACOS

These tacos provide a nice veggie and protein boost to your meal. This simple recipe is full of flavor and will leave you completely satisfied without weighing you down. Coconut aminos are used instead of soy sauce. They taste exactly like their counterpart, but are Paleo-approved and much better for you!

SERVES 6–8

1½ lbs (680 g) flank steak, cut into 2 x ½–inch (50 x 12–mm)-wide strips

2 tbsp (18 g) coconut sugar

2 cloves garlic, minced

1 tbsp (15 ml) sesame oil

½ cup (120 ml) coconut aminos

1 tbsp (6 g) grated ginger

2 cups (113 g) cauliflower rice

1 red bell pepper, sliced

Head of butter lettuce, separated into leaves

Pickled jalapeños, optional

Sliced avocado, optional

¼ cup (4 g) chopped fresh cilantro

1 lime, sliced

Put the steak in a resealable plastic bag. Add the sugar, garlic, sesame oil, coconut aminos and ginger to the bag, then shake the bag to coat the meat. Marinate the meat in the refrigerator for at least 1 hour, or up to 6 hours.

When you are ready to make the tacos, preheat the oven to 400°F (204°C), and line a baking sheet with parchment paper. Arrange the cauliflower rice and bell pepper on one side of the sheet pan and the marinated steak on the other side. It's OK if some of the meat is overlapping.

Cook the meat and vegetables for 10 to 15 minutes, or until the bell pepper can be easily pierced with a fork and the internal temperature of the steak reaches 130°F (54°C) on an instant-read thermometer. Remove the pan from the oven and let the beef and vegetables cool for a couple of minutes.

To assemble the tacos, scoop some of the cauliflower rice and bell peppers into the bottom of a leaf of lettuce, then top it with a few strips of meat and the pickled jalapeños and avocado, if using. Garnish with fresh chopped cilantro and a good squeeze of lime!

APPLE-DIJON STUFFED PORK LOIN

We have this cute little German restaurant in town, and one of its menu options is breaded pork, which comes with a side of applesauce that you are supposed to spread on top. I never thought about that as a combo, but boy does it work. This is my take on that meal, and it makes for an unbelievable Paleo dinner sure to impress anyone who tries it as much as the German restaurant impressed me! The veggies and sauce in this recipe are the same as for the Mustard-Roasted Vegetables (page 95) that I love so much.

SERVES 8

2 lbs (907 g) pork loin

1 Pink Lady apple, cored and cut into 12 thin slices

½ cup (124 g) Dijon mustard, divided

⅓ cup (9 g) chopped fresh rosemary

3¼ tsp (19 g) sea salt, divided

3 tbsp (45 ml) avocado oil

1 tbsp (4 g) dried thyme

1 tbsp (15 ml) apple cider vinegar

½ tsp ground black pepper

1 lb (454 g) cauliflower florets

2 medium yellow onions, roughly chopped

1 lb (454 g) Brussels sprouts, halved

2 Japanese sweet potatoes, diced

2 fennel bulbs, quartered

Fresh rosemary sprigs

Preheat the oven to 450°F (232°C). While the oven is preheating, take a sharp knife and slice down the middle of the pork horizontally. Don't slice all the way through the pork, as you will be stuffing the apples into it and you want them to stay put.

Tuck the apple slices, in a single layer, into the pocket you cut into the pork. Rub ¼ cup (62 g) of the Dijon mustard over the entire piece of meat. Sprinkle the rosemary and 2 teaspoons (12 g) of the salt over the top of the pork. Reduce the oven temperature to 325°F (162°C). Roast the pork for 30 minutes.

While the pork is roasting, prepare the vegetables. In a small bowl, whisk the remaining ¼ cup (62 g) of Dijon, the remaining 1¼ teaspoons (7 g) of salt, the oil, thyme, vinegar and pepper until fully combined. In a large bowl, combine the cauliflower, onions, Brussels sprouts, sweet potatoes and fennel. Pour the mustard mixture over the vegetables, and toss to coat them completely.

After the pork has roasted for 30 minutes, arrange the vegetable mixture around the roast, and return the pan to the oven for another 20 to 25 minutes, or until the internal temperature of the pork reaches 150°F (65°C) on an instant-read thermometer. Remove the pan from the oven, lightly cover the meat with foil and let the meat rest for 5 minutes.

For serving, slice the meat and garnish it with the rosemary sprigs.

SHRIMP PUTTANESCA

This dish is a fantastic, healthy, Paleo alternative to traditional Italian puttanesca. You can substitute zucchini noodles or chopped chard for the spaghetti squash. I enjoy this meal hot or cold, and I sometimes add a sprinkle of red pepper flakes to kick up the heat a bit!

SERVES 4–6

1 large spaghetti squash, cut in half horizontally and seeded

1½ tbsp (21 g) ghee or oil of preference, for greasing

1 (14-oz [397-g]) can water-packed quartered artichoke hearts, drained

¼ cup (34 g) capers, drained

½ cup (90 g) Kalamata olives

1 pint (275 g) cherry tomatoes, halved

1 large Japanese sweet potato, diced

8 cloves garlic, halved

1 lb (454 g) raw medium shrimp, peeled and deveined

Fresh parsley sprigs

Red pepper flakes, optional

Preheat the oven to 425°F (218°C). Arrange the spaghetti squash, cut-side down, on a baking sheet. Bake the squash for 30 minutes, then transfer it to a plate to cool. When the squash is cool enough to handle, scoop out the squash strands with a fork and set them aside.

Reduce the oven temperature to 385°F (196°C). Grease the baking sheet with ghee or oil, and put the artichokes, capers, olives, tomatoes, sweet potato and garlic on the baking sheet. Bake the vegetables for 20 minutes.

Remove the pan from the oven, and add the spaghetti squash and shrimp to it. Toss to combine the vegetables, spaghetti squash and shrimp. Return the pan to the oven and cook the mixture for 5 to 7 minutes, or until the shrimp is pink and opaque in color. Garnish the dish with the parsley and the red pepper flakes, if using.

LEMON-GARLIC HALIBUT WITH ROASTED ASPARAGUS

This simple dish is sure to delight everyone around the table. Light and refreshing, this Paleo dinner won't leave you feeling ill afterward. Broccoli or cauliflower are good vegetable substitutes if asparagus is not in season.

SERVES 4–6

2 lbs (907 g) asparagus spears

1 tbsp (15 ml) extra virgin olive oil

2 tbsp (12 g) lemon zest, divided

2 lbs (907 g) fresh halibut fillets

2 tsp (12 g) sea salt

½ cup (113 g) ghee

4 cloves garlic, minced

2 tbsp (30 ml) fresh lemon juice

1 tsp ground black pepper

Fresh parsley sprigs, optional

Preheat the oven to 400°F (204°C), and line a sheet pan with parchment paper.

Spread the asparagus across the pan and drizzle it with the olive oil and 1 tablespoon (6 g) of the lemon zest. Pat the halibut dry and place the fillets on top of the asparagus. Sprinkle the salt over the fillets.

Put the ghee in a small bowl and microwave it for 30 seconds, or until it is melted. Add the garlic, lemon juice and pepper to the ghee and stir to combine. Brush the mixture onto the halibut, then bake the fish and asparagus for 15 minutes, or until the halibut is light golden brown on top.

For serving, garnish the fish with the remaining 1 tablespoon (6 g) of lemon zest and the parsley, if using.

CRISPY BAKED FISH 'N' FRIES

Few meals are as tasty as a good ol' basket of fish and chips! You wouldn't think there could be a healthy Paleo replacement for the battered and deep-fried classic, but this meal is filled with healthy fats, protein and antioxidants. You will leave the table feeling completely satisfied. White fish works best with this recipe. I prefer cod, but halibut, flounder or tilapia will also work. Pro tip: The key to enjoying this dish is to dip everything in the tartar sauce.

SERVES 6

FOR THE FISH AND FRIES

3 Japanese sweet potatoes, cut into ½-inch (12-mm)-wide strips

1½ tbsp (21 g) ghee or oil of preference, for greasing

1 egg

1 tbsp (3 g) dried dill

1 tsp sea salt, plus more for the potatoes

1 cup (112 g) superfine almond flour

¼ cup (32 g) tapioca starch

1⅓ tsp (1 g) dried parsley

½ tsp ground black pepper

6 large cod fillets, halved vertically

Avocado oil spray

Juice of ¼ lemon

Fresh parsley sprigs

FOR THE TARTAR SAUCE

½ cup (119 g) Paleo mayonnaise (I like Primal Kitchen or Tessemae's.)

1 dill pickle, finely chopped

1½ tbsp (23 ml) fresh lemon juice

⅔ tsp chopped fresh dill

For the fish and fries, put the sweet potatoes into a bowl of water while you make the fish; this helps release the starch and makes the fries crispy.

Preheat the oven to 400°F (204°C), and grease a sheet pan or line it with parchment paper. Whisk the egg in a shallow bowl. In another shallow bowl, mix the dill, 1 teaspoon of salt, almond flour, tapioca starch, parsley and pepper.

Dredge the fish by first dipping it in the egg on both sides, then coating it with the almond flour mix. Place each fillet on one side of the sheet pan as you coat it.

Drain the potatoes and pat them dry with a paper towel. Arrange the potato pieces on the other side of the sheet pan, and coat them with the oil spray. Sprinkle a generous amount of salt over the fries.

Cook the fish and fries for 20 minutes, or until everything on the sheet pan is golden brown.

Prepare the tartar sauce while the fish and fries are baking. Combine the mayonnaise, pickle, lemon juice and dill in a small bowl.

For serving, plate the fish and fries and garnish it with the lemon juice, parsley and prepared tartar sauce.

SWEDISH MEATBALLS

When I was younger, my favorite TV dinner was Swedish meatballs. We didn't have TV dinners very often, but when we did, I chose the meatballs every single time. I haven't had that TV dinner in years, but when I make these, I always think back to my childhood days. These Paleo-friendly Swedish meatballs trump any TV dinner out there. They pair well with sweet potatoes or even spaghetti squash.

SERVES 6

FOR THE MEATBALLS

2 lbs (907 g) ground beef

1 egg

1 tsp ground allspice

1 tsp ground nutmeg

1 tsp sea salt

1 tbsp (2 g) dried parsley

1 lb (454 g) cauliflower florets

Fresh Italian parsley sprigs

FOR THE GRAVY

1½ cups (360 ml) bone broth

2 tbsp (28 g) ghee

⅛ tsp ground allspice

⅛ tsp ground nutmeg

1 tsp dried parsley

1 tbsp (8 g) arrowroot powder mixed with 2 tbsp (30 ml) water

For the meatballs, preheat the oven to 375°F (190°C), and line your sheet pan with parchment paper.

In a mixing bowl, combine the beef, egg, allspice, nutmeg, salt and parsley, using your hands. Roll the mixture into 1½-inch (4-cm) balls, and arrange the balls on one half of the sheet pan, making sure that the meatballs aren't touching. Arrange the cauliflower florets on the other half of the sheet pan.

Bake the meatballs and cauliflower for 20 minutes, or until the meatballs are browned and the cauliflower is fork tender. If necessary, remove the meatballs from the pan to a bowl covered with foil to keep them warm, and cook the cauliflower for 3 to 5 more minutes, until it becomes tender.

Prepare the gravy while the meatballs and cauliflower are cooking. Put the broth, ghee, allspice, nutmeg and parsley in a small pot. Bring the mixture to a boil over medium-high heat, then reduce the heat until the mixture is simmering.

Whisking constantly, pour the arrowroot mixture (slurry) into the broth. Continue to stir until the gravy becomes thick, about 2 to 3 minutes. Remove the gravy from the heat, and set it aside.

For serving, transfer the cauliflower to a serving bowl, top it with the meatballs, then pour the gravy over the top. Garnish the dish with the parsley sprigs.

Sides

AW, SHEET, HERE COME THE SIDES!

This chapter highlights my absolute favorite Paleo sheet pan side dishes. Many people think that Paleo eating is all about meat, but in our house, every meal is served with a nutritious side dish. Sometimes more sides are on our plates than meat! Each one of these side dishes will send your taste buds straight to Flavortown.

ROASTED ROSEMARY-GARLIC CARROTS

Run, don't walk, to make this fantastic Paleo side dish. The trick to these roasted carrots is letting them cook first for a bit just plain and then adding all the delicious seasoning goodness to them. These carrots make a superb side dish to my Peppercorn Balsamic Tri-Tip (page 38) or the Crispy Baked Fish 'n' Fries (page 78). They are also a fantastic addition to any holiday meal!

SERVES 4

10–12 large rainbow carrots

Avocado oil spray

Pinch of salt

½ cup (113 g) ghee

½ shallot, finely chopped

2 cloves garlic, minced

1 sprig fresh rosemary, plus more for garnish

Preheat the oven to 400°F (204°C). Place the carrots in a single layer on your sheet pan. Spray the carrots with the avocado oil and sprinkle the salt over them. Put the carrots into the oven, and cook them for 20 minutes.

In a small saucepan, melt the ghee. Add the shallot, garlic and the sprig of rosemary. Let the mixture simmer over low heat while the carrots cook. After 20 minutes, flip the carrots and generously brush the ghee mixture on each one. Return the carrots to the oven and cook for another 20 minutes, or until they are easily pierced with a fork.

Garnish the carrots with the rosemary.

BUFFALO ROASTED CAULIFLOWER

My favorite side, this dish is simple, satisfying and full of flavor! Add as much or as little hot sauce to satisfy your taste buds. Serve this with your favorite protein. We love it with Buttermilk-Drenched Caveman Pops (page 61) and even, dare I say it, the Rich and Savory Sausage Patties (page 22).

SERVES 4

FOR THE BUFFALO RANCH SAUCE

1 cup (235 g) Paleo mayonnaise
(I like Primal Kitchen or Tessemae's.)

¼ cup (60 ml) Paleo-friendly
hot sauce

1 tsp onion powder

½ tsp garlic powder

½ tsp dried rosemary

½ tsp dried dill

FOR THE CAULIFLOWER

2 lbs (907 g) cauliflower florets

1 cup (240 ml) Buffalo Ranch Sauce

Fresh parsley sprigs

Preheat the oven to 425°F (218°C).

For the sauce, in a small bowl, whisk together the mayonnaise, hot sauce, onion powder, garlic powder, rosemary and dill until it's blended well.

For the cauliflower, place the florets in a bowl and pour the buffalo sauce over them. Toss until all of the cauliflower is well coated with the buffalo sauce. The remaining sauce may be refrigerated in an airtight container for up to 2 weeks.

Spread the cauliflower evenly on the prepared pan. Roast the cauliflower for 10 minutes. Toss the cauliflower to ensure even cooking, then return the pan to the oven for another 10 to 15 minutes, or until the cauliflower is fork tender. For serving, garnish the cauliflower with the parsley sprigs.

SPICY CRISPY GREEN BEANS WITH PANCETTA

I've never been a fan of green beans, until now. Pancetta, which is a cured ham, pairs perfectly with the crispy beans. Serve these at your next holiday party, as they will be a sure win. If green beans aren't available, substitute asparagus or Brussels sprouts.

SERVES 6

1 lb (454 g) green beans, trimmed

1 tsp sweet paprika

1 tsp garlic powder

½ tsp chili powder

1 tsp sea salt

4 oz (113 g) chopped pancetta

1 egg, whisked

1 cup (112 g) superfine almond flour

Preheat the oven to 400°F (204°C). Line a sheet pan with parchment paper.

In a large mixing bowl, use your hands to combine well the green beans, paprika, garlic powder, chili powder, salt, pancetta, egg and almond flour.

Spread the bean mixture on the prepared pan, then rearrange the beans to make sure none are overlapping. Put the sheet pan into the oven and cook the beans for 10 minutes. Stir the beans, then cook them for another 10 to 15 minutes, or until the beans are golden brown.

ROSEMARY-BALSAMIC MUSHROOMS AND ROASTED TOMATOES

There are few things that are better than roasted tomatoes! The skin gets all blistered and they turn slightly sweet. Yum! Add mushrooms, and you have a match made in heaven. Heirloom tomatoes, when in season, are best for this recipe, but you could use any tomatoes. This combo can be added to almost anything to make a complete Paleo meal. My favorite ways to use this dish are over spaghetti squash or Spanish cauliflower rice or blended into a tomato soup.

SERVES 4

2 lbs (907 g) heirloom tomatoes, quartered

12 oz (340 g) sliced mushrooms

1 tbsp (3 g) dried oregano

1½ tbsp (2 g) chopped fresh rosemary

1½ tsp (9 g) sea salt

2 tbsp (30 ml) extra virgin olive oil

¼ cup (60 ml) balsamic vinegar

Preheat the oven to 425° F (218°C). Arrange the tomatoes and mushrooms on a sheet pan. Sprinkle the oregano, rosemary and salt over the top. Drizzle the olive oil and balsamic over the vegetables, then toss them with your hands or a pair of tongs to evenly coat them.

Roast the tomatoes and mushrooms for 15 minutes, or until the mushrooms are a dark golden brown. Remove the pan from the oven, and toss the vegetables one more time to mix the flavors well.

> **NOTE:** I like to makes batches of these roasted veggies ahead. I freeze them in resealable plastic bags, then reheat them on a night when I'm busy but still want to get in a delicious Paleo dinner.

BROCCOLI TATER TOTS

These broccoli tots are perfect for making ahead of time and packing into lunches or taking on-the-go for a healthy Paleo snack. You can also eat them with dinner for a complete meal. Don't forget to dip all this tot goodness into the aioli!

SERVES 4

FOR THE TATER TOTS

3 cups (273 g) finely chopped broccoli (I use the food processor.)

2 cups (266 g) grated Japanese purple sweet potatoes

3 eggs

2 tbsp (16 g) tapioca starch

1 tsp garlic powder

1 tsp dried minced onion

⅛ tsp ground black pepper

½ tsp sea salt

1 tbsp (5 g) nutritional yeast, optional

FOR THE LEMON-TARRAGON AIOLI

1 cup (235 g) Paleo mayonnaise (I like Primal Kitchen or Tessemae's.)

Juice of ½ lemon

1 tbsp (2 g) dried tarragon

For the tots, preheat the oven to 400°F (204°C), and line a sheet pan with parchment paper.

Place the broccoli and sweet potatoes in a medium-sized mixing bowl. Add the eggs, tapioca starch, garlic powder, onion, pepper, salt and nutritional yeast, if using. Mix well until everything in the bowl is combined.

Scoop a handful of the broccoli–sweet potato mixture and shape it into a "tot" shape, about 1½ inches (4 cm) long. Place it on the prepared pan. Repeat with the remaining mixture; you should get about 18 tots. Put the sheet pan into the oven and bake the tots for 20 minutes, or until the tots are golden brown and a bit crispy.

Prepare the aioli while the tots cook. Whisk together the mayonnaise, lemon juice and tarragon in a small bowl and set aside. Once the broccoli tots are done, plate and dip.

NOTE: Leftover aioli can be stored in an airtight container in the refrigerator for 1½ weeks. It will need to be stirred before each use.

MUSTARD-ROASTED VEGETABLES

Mustard is my favorite condiment, so when I'm looking for a healthy, tasty side dish, it only seems right to smother veggies with a mustard sauce! Did you know that mustard has a lot of health benefits, such as stimulating and aiding in digestion and inhibiting cancer cell growth? And that's just naming a few! The vegetables I call for are available year-round, but feel free to make your own veggie medley with your seasonal favorites. I love these so much that I use this recipe with the Apple-Dijon Stuffed Pork Loin (page 73).

SERVES 6

1 lb (454 g) cauliflower florets

2 medium yellow onions, roughly chopped

1 lb (454 g) Brussels sprouts, halved

2 Japanese sweet potatoes, diced

2 fennel bulbs, quartered

3 tbsp (45 ml) avocado oil

¼ cup (62 g) Dijon mustard

1 tbsp (15 ml) apple cider vinegar

1 tbsp (4 g) dried thyme

1¼ tsp (7 g) sea salt

½ tsp ground black pepper

Preheat the oven to 425°F (218°C). Line a baking sheet with parchment paper.

Combine the cauliflower, onions, Brussels sprouts, potatoes and fennel in a large bowl. In a small bowl, combine the avocado oil, mustard, vinegar, thyme, salt and pepper and whisk until it's fully combined. Pour the mustard mixture over the veggies and toss to coat the veggies with the sauce.

Spread the veggie mixture in a single layer on the prepared baking sheet. Roast the mixture for 20 minutes, stir, then bake for another 15 to 20 minutes, or until the potatoes can be easily pierced with a fork and the vegetables are tender and golden.

"FRIED" CAULIFLOWER RICE

This is a fun take on fried rice using real, fresh, wholesome ingredients. The cauliflower rice is a great alternative to regular rice. This is a favorite of mine because of its simplicity. Just toss everything onto the sheet pan and let your oven do its thing! This is spectacular with the Crispy Beef and Broccoli (page 49).

SERVES 4

1½ tbsp (21 g) ghee or oil of preference, for greasing

2 (10-oz [283-g]) bags cauliflower rice

2 large carrots, diced

1 rib celery, diced

2 cloves garlic, minced

1 tsp minced fresh ginger

3 tbsp (45 ml) coconut aminos

½ tsp fish sauce

2 eggs, whisked

2 green onions, sliced

Preheat the oven to 375°F (190°C), and grease a sheet pan with ghee or olive oil.

In a large bowl, mix together the cauliflower rice, carrots, celery, garlic, ginger, coconut aminos and fish sauce. Evenly spread the mixture on the prepared pan. Place the pan in the oven and cook the rice for 15 minutes.

Remove the sheet pan from the oven, pour the eggs over the top and stir to combine them with the rice mixture. Return the pan to the oven, and cook the rice for 10 minutes, or until the eggs are cooked and no longer runny. Garnish the rice with the green onions.

ROASTED BRUSSELS SPROUTS WITH BACON AND CHILI VINAIGRETTE

This is one of my absolute favorite recipes to showcase how scrumptious Paleo eating can be! A lot of people think that Paleo food is super bland, because it uses basic ingredients. But I'm here to tell you: You are oh-so-wrong. These roasted Brussels sprouts are a game-changer, and friends have told me that this was the dish that made them love Brussels sprouts and eating healthier. We enjoy this side with the Jalapeño-Popper Stuffed Chicken (page 42).

SERVES 6

FOR THE BRUSSELS SPROUTS

2 lbs (907 g) Brussels sprouts, halved

1 tbsp (15 ml) olive oil

4 slices sugar-free bacon, chopped

2 tbsp (17 g) capers

½ cup (58 g) chopped walnuts

Pinch of salt

FOR THE CHILI VINAIGRETTE

1 tbsp (7 g) red pepper flakes

1 tbsp (15 ml) red wine vinegar

¼ cup (60 ml) olive oil

2 tsp (10 ml) honey

For the Brussels sprouts, preheat the oven to 400°F (204°C), and line a sheet pan with parchment paper.

In a large bowl, toss the sprouts with the oil. Evenly spread the Brussels sprouts on the prepared pan. Place the bacon on top of the Brussels sprouts. Put the baking sheet into the oven, and cook the sprouts for 20 minutes, or until they are deep brown in color and look crispy.

Prepare the vinaigrette while the Brussels sprouts are roasting. In a small bowl, whisk together the red pepper flakes, vinegar, olive oil and honey.

When the Brussels sprouts are cooked, stir in the capers and walnuts right on the sheet pan. Sprinkle the sprouts with the salt. For serving, drizzle the vinaigrette over the roasted Brussels sprouts.

> **NOTE:** I like to plate my Brussels sprouts before drizzling the vinaigrette over them. This allows me to adjust the amount of vinaigrette for each serving, since everyone has a different tolerance for hot foods.

SMOTHERED JAMAICAN JERK ASPARAGUS AND CARROTS

"Whoa, whoa, whoa!" That's exactly what my family said when they tried these for the first time. You might want to cook two sheet pans of this recipe, because the asparagus and carrots go fast. You can double the seasoning recipe and store half of it in an airtight container. Jamaican seasoning rocks on chicken, fish and steak.

SERVES 4

FOR THE JAMAICAN SEASONING

1 tbsp (8 g) garlic powder

1½ tsp (4 g) onion powder

2 tsp (1 g) dried parsley

1½ tsp (3 g) ground allspice

2 tsp (1 g) cayenne pepper

½ tsp ground cinnamon

1 tsp smoked paprika

½ tsp red pepper flakes

2 tsp (12 g) sea salt

1 tsp ground black pepper

2 tsp (6 g) coconut sugar

FOR THE VEGGIES

1 bunch rainbow carrots

1 lb (454 g) asparagus

2 tbsp (30 ml) avocado oil

For the seasoning, in a small bowl, mix together the garlic powder, onion powder, parsley, allspice, cayenne, cinnamon, paprika, red pepper flakes, salt, pepper and sugar. Set aside the mixture.

For the veggies, preheat the oven to 400°F (204°C), and line a baking sheet with parchment paper.

Place the carrots and asparagus on the baking sheet and drizzle them with the oil. Sprinkle the Jamaican seasoning over the top, and mix with your hands or tongs to make sure everything is well-coated. Put the sheet pan into the oven, and roast the vegetables for 25 minutes, or until the carrots are fork tender.

BACON-WRAPPED ARTICHOKE HEARTS

I am mildly obsessed with all things artichokes. OK, OK, I lied! I'm *very* obsessed with all things artichokes. I even have ten artichoke plants in my front yard, and our home is known as the "artichoke house" in our neighborhood. Jam-packed full of antioxidants, artichokes are kind of a hidden gem. I love to serve these when I host a party or throw them over a big bowl of mixed greens.

SERVES 16–20

1 (14-oz [397-g]) can water-packed artichoke hearts, drained

12 oz (340 g) sugar-free bacon, each slice cut in half

Fresh rosemary sprigs

Preheat the oven to 425°F (218°C), and line a sheet pan with parchment paper.

Dry the artichokes with paper towels. Wrap a piece of the bacon around an artichoke heart, then place it on the sheet pan. Repeat until all the artichoke hearts have been wrapped in bacon.

Roast the bacon-wrapped artichokes for 15 minutes, or until the bacon is crispy. For serving, garnish each piece with a sprig of the rosemary.

MINI SWEET POTATO REUBEN STACKS

These mini Reuben stacks have all the flavor of one of the best sandwiches out there, but without any of the grains and gut-bloating carbs. These poppable little stacks are perfect for lunch boxes, or for dinner with a side salad, if you are looking for something lighter to eat.

SERVES 4

FOR THE DRESSING

½ cup (119 g) Paleo mayonnaise (I like Primal Kitchen or Tessemae's.)

¼ cup (58 g) sugar-free ketchup

¼ cup (36 g) finely chopped dill pickle

1 tsp onion powder

1 tsp garlic powder

FOR THE SAUERKRAUT

1 head cabbage

1 tbsp (18 g) salt

FOR THE REUBENS

1 large sweet potato, cut into ⅛-inch (4-mm) slices

Avocado oil

8 oz (227 g) thinly sliced pastrami or corned beef

1 cup (33 g) microgreens

For the dressing, in a small bowl, mix together the mayonnaise, ketchup, pickle, onion powder and garlic powder. Set aside the dressing.

For the sauerkraut, shred the head of cabbage and place it in a large bowl. Add the salt and mix together. Let it sit for 10 to 15 minutes. After 15 minutes, massage and squeeze the cabbage. When liquid comes out, it's ready. Taste and see if it needs more salt. You can store this in a jar in your fridge for months!

For the Reubens, preheat the oven to 415°F (212°C) and line a quarter sheet pan with parchment paper. Arrange the sweet potato slices on the prepared pan, then drizzle them with a little of the oil. Bake the slices for 10 minutes.

Remove the pan from the oven, and flip over each sweet potato. Spoon a little dressing on top of each sweet potato slice, then add a piece of pastrami and a spoonful of sauerkraut. Return the pan to the oven, and bake the Reubens for another 10 minutes, or until the sauerkraut starts to brown a bit.

For serving, drizzle a little more dressing on each stack, then top the stacks with the microgreens.

ROASTED ARTICHOKE-PESTO CABBAGE STEAKS

A simple and delicious side like these cabbage wedges is a great way to add flavor to your meal. The artichokes are the star of the show and add a creamy element to this wonderful Paleo side dish. Serve with the Lemon-Garlic Halibut with Roasted Asparagus (page 77).

SERVES 6

FOR THE CABBAGE

1 large head cabbage, cut, with the stem intact, into ½-inch (12-mm) slices

FOR THE ARTICHOKE-BASIL PESTO

1 bunch (24 g) fresh basil

1 clove garlic, minced

1 tsp lemon zest

½ cup (120 ml) avocado oil

Juice of ½ lemon

½ cup (84 g) water-packed quartered artichoke hearts, drained

Pinch of salt

1 tbsp (8 g) pine nuts, optional

For the cabbage, preheat the oven to 400°F (204°C), and line a baking sheet with parchment paper. Arrange the cabbage steaks on the prepared pan.

For the pesto, in a blender, blend the basil, garlic, lemon zest, oil, lemon juice, artichoke hearts, salt and pine nuts, if using, until the mixture is smooth. Using half of the pesto, spread pesto onto each slice of cabbage, then bake the steaks for 10 minutes.

Remove the sheet pan from the oven, and spread the remaining half of the pesto over each slice. Return the pan to the oven, and cook the steaks for another 10 to 15 minutes, or until the cabbage wedges are fork tender.

HONEY-GLAZED BRUSSELS SPROUTS

Brussels sprouts always have had a bad rap. Why did our grandparents think they would be delicious boiled until they were soggy?! Luckily, most of us know that Brussels sprouts are indeed scrumptious when cooked and seasoned correctly. This recipe is exceptionally good: a little sweet, with a little zing from the garlic and paprika.

SERVES 8

2 lbs (907 g) Brussels sprouts, halved

2 tbsp (30 ml) oil of preference

3 cloves garlic, crushed

1½ tsp (3 g) sweet paprika

1 tsp sea salt, plus more for serving

¼ cup (60 ml) honey, plus more for serving

Preheat the oven to 450°F (232°C), and line a sheet pan with parchment paper. On the paper, use tongs to toss the Brussels sprouts with the oil, garlic, paprika, salt and honey.

Place the sheet pan in the oven and cook the Brussels sprouts for 7 to 10 minutes, or until they are crispy. For serving, sprinkle the sprouts with a bit more salt and drizzle them with more honey.

SWEET POTATO CROSTINI WITH PEARS AND PISTACHIOS

This side is more on the sweet side than savory, but who says every side dish needs to be savory? Crostini is usually done with bread, but the sweet potato is a great alternative to the gluten option and much healthier, too!

SERVES 6

2 medium sweet potatoes, cut into ⅛-inch (4-mm) slices

¼ tsp sea salt

2 pears, sliced

3 tbsp (45 ml) melted coconut oil

Honey, for drizzling

Dash of ground cinnamon

½ cup (62 g) chopped pistachios

Preheat the oven to 450°F (232°C), and line a baking sheet with parchment paper.

Spread the sweet potatoes onto the baking sheet, and sprinkle the salt on them. Lay a couple slices of pear onto each potato, then drizzle the oil over the top. Roast the crostini for 15 minutes, or until the pears and potatoes are fork tender.

For serving, drizzle the crostini with honey, a sprinkle of the cinnamon and the pistachios.

TANDOORI MIXED VEGGIES

Usually tandoori recipes are made in a tandoor, the traditional clay and brick oven used throughout India to cook foods over very high heat. But I'm pretty sure most of you don't own one. I sure don't! These roasted veggies are what your Paleo dreams are made of.

SERVES 6–8

1 lb (454 g) baby carrots

1 red onion, chopped

¾ lb (340 g) cauliflower florets

2 bell peppers, sliced

1 large sweet potato, diced

½ tsp coriander

½ tsp turmeric

1 tsp sweet paprika

½ tsp ground cinnamon

¼ tsp ground cumin

⅛ tsp dry mustard

⅛ tsp ground nutmeg

1 tsp sea salt

1½ tbsp (23 ml) fresh lime juice

2 tbsp (30 ml) oil of preference

½ cup (120 ml) plain almond or coconut yogurt (I like Kite Hill.)

Preheat the oven to 425°F (218°C), and line a baking sheet with parchment paper.

In a large bowl, combine the carrots, onion, cauliflower, bell peppers and sweet potato. In a small ramekin, mix together the coriander, turmeric, paprika, cinnamon, cumin, mustard, nutmeg and salt. Pour the seasoning mix over the bowl of vegetables, then add the lime juice, oil and yogurt. Toss until all the veggies are well-coated. Spread the veggies out on the prepared baking sheet, and put the pan in the oven.

Let the vegetables roast for 15 minutes, mix them up with a pair of tongs, then cook them for another 15 to 20 minutes, or until the veggies are fork tender and browned.

Dessert
YOU DESERVE IT!

What's a cookbook without desserts? Boring. Just kidding, but I feel like every great cookbook has a dessert section. And for good reason: Desserts are amazing! However, when changing to a Paleo diet, desserts are usually the first thing to which you say, "Sayonara!" But—in moderation—you can enjoy some pretty spectacular healthier options for when you feel like you want to eat something delectable.

PIZOOKIE

Remember when pizookies were all the rage back in the early 2000s? They were in every restaurant. Now you can enjoy a much healthier version of this dessert guilt-free! Serve your pizookie with some purchased Paleo-friendly ice cream or make your own banana nice cream.

SERVES 10–12

⅔ cup (147 g) ghee, softened

¾ cup (109 g) coconut sugar

1 tsp vanilla extract

1 egg

2¼ cups (252 g) superfine almond flour

½ cup (64 g) tapioca flour

½ tsp baking soda

1 cup (170 g) Paleo-friendly semi-sweet chocolate chips (Enjoy Life is a good brand.)

Preheat the oven to 350°F (177°C), and line a quarter sheet pan with parchment paper.

With an electric mixer, cream together the ghee and sugar in a large mixing bowl. Add the vanilla and egg and mix again. Add the almond flour, tapioca flour and baking soda to the bowl, and mix on low until they are fully combined with the ghee mixture. Scrape down the sides, if needed. Fold in the chocolate chips with a rubber spatula.

Evenly spread the cookie dough on the prepared pan, patting the dough with your hands into a rectangle 9 x 12 inches (23 x 30.5 cm).

Bake the pizookie for 10 to 12 minutes, or until it's golden brown. Cut the cookie into squares and serve warm, or allow the pizookie to cool in the pan.

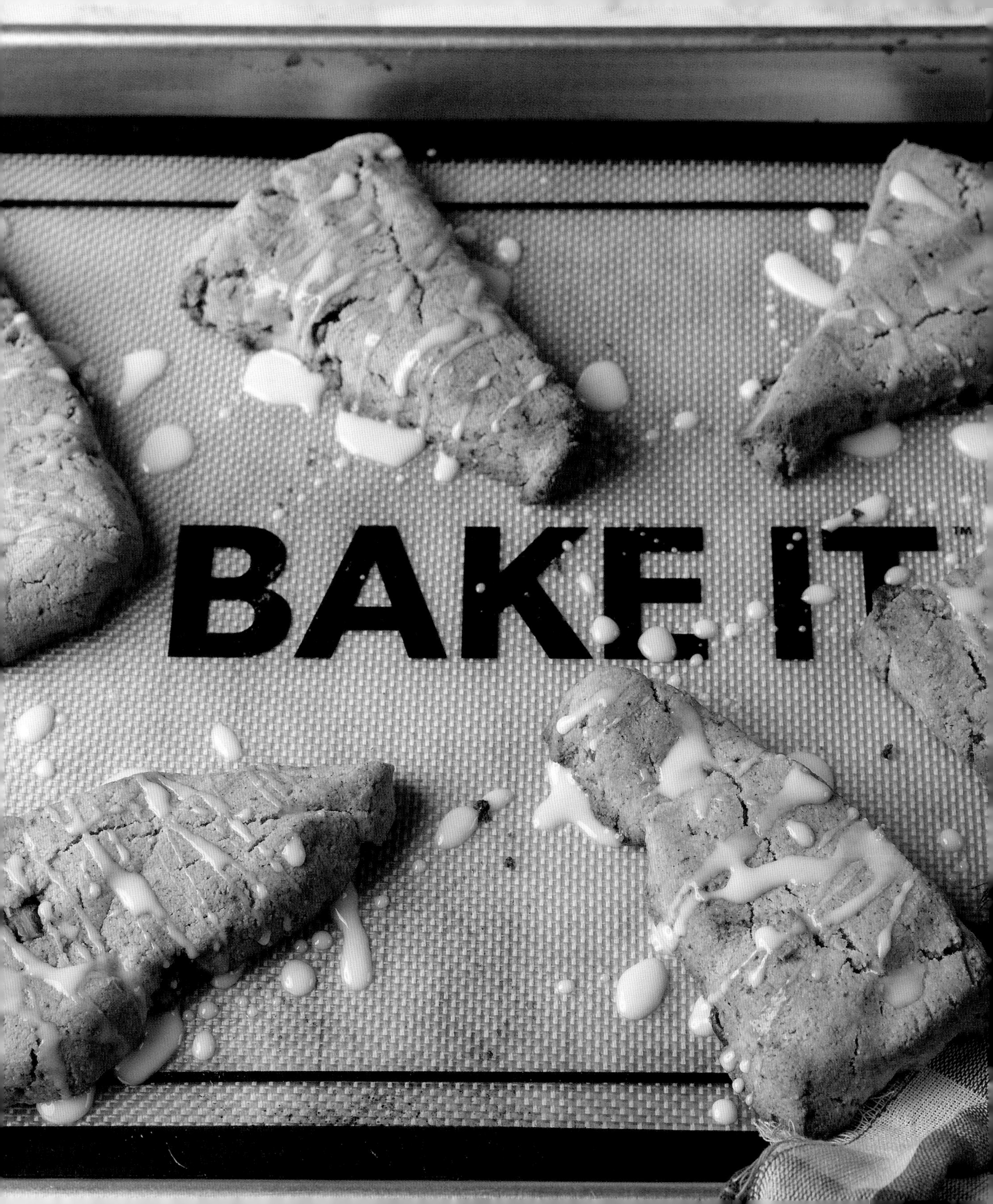
BAKE IT™

PECAN "MONKEY BREAD" SCONES

I'm sure you all think of breakfast when you hear the word scone, but let's be real with ourselves. We could all eat a scone at any time of day! This recipe is a fun twist on monkey bread, and it pairs well with afternoon delights, such as coffee or tea. To further simplify this recipe, drizzle the scones with honey instead of the glaze.

SERVES 8

FOR THE SCONES

1 cup (112 g) superfine almond flour

¼ cup (28 g) cassava flour

3 tbsp (27 g) coconut sugar

1 tsp baking powder

1¼ tsp (3 g) ground cinnamon

Pinch of salt

1 egg

4 tbsp (60 ml) melted ghee

¼ cup (60 ml) unsweetened almond milk

1 tsp vanilla extract

½ cup (55 g) chopped pecans

FOR THE GLAZE

1 tbsp (15 ml) melted ghee

2 tbsp (30 ml) unsweetened almond milk

4 tbsp (36 g) coconut sugar

For the scones, preheat the oven to 350°F (177°C), and line a baking sheet with parchment paper.

In a large mixing bowl, mix together the almond flour, cassava flour, sugar, baking powder, cinnamon and salt. Make a well in the center of the flour mixture, put the egg in the well and whisk it into the mixture. Stir in the ghee, almond milk and vanilla, then fold in the pecans.

Place the dough in the middle of the sheet pan and spread it into a ½-inch (12-mm)-thick circle. Cut the dough into 8 wedges and arrange them, 2 inches (5 cm) apart, on the baking sheet. Bake the scones for 20 minutes. Turn off the oven, and leave the scones inside it for 10 minutes.

Prepare the glaze while the scones are resting in the oven. In a small bowl, whisk together the melted ghee, almond milk and sugar. Drizzle the glaze over the scones.

OOEY-GOOEY AVOCADO BROWNIES

These Paleo brownies are super fudgy and make a great low-carb, nutrient-dense evening dessert. Whip these up if you are in the mood for some chocolaty, healthy Paleo goodness. You can store leftovers in an airtight container in the refrigerator for up to a week; however, I highly doubt they will last that long. We enjoy pairing these with Paleo-friendly ice cream.

SERVES 12

½ cup (120 ml) melted coconut oil

1 tbsp (15 ml) melted ghee

⅔ cup (96 g) coconut sugar

1 ripe avocado, mashed

⅓ cup (28 g) cocoa powder

¾ cup (84 g) superfine almond flour

1½ tsp (6 g) baking powder

2 eggs

½ cup (85 g) Paleo-friendly semi-sweet chocolate chips

Preheat the oven to 350°F (177°C), and line a quarter sheet pan with parchment paper.

In a large mixing bowl, use an electric mixer to beat together the coconut oil, ghee, sugar, avocado, cocoa, almond flour, baking powder and eggs just until the mixture is smooth. Do not overmix.

Fold in the chocolate chips, reserving a few to garnish the top, if you wish. Pour the batter onto the baking sheet and smooth it out evenly. Bake the brownies for 25 minutes, or until the edges start to separate from the sides of the pan. Let the brownies cool in the pan for 10 minutes before you slice them.

STRAWBERRY SWIRL ALMOND MERINGUES

These light and airy morsels are a fun little treat to have when you want something sweet, but not overly sweet. The method is fairly easy, and the results are superb. Be patient, as the meringues need to completely cool in the oven before you take them out. You can make these in the evening and let them sit overnight in the oven to be ready to enjoy the next day.

SERVES 20

FOR THE STRAWBERRY SAUCE
8 oz (227 g) strawberries, pureed

2 tbsp (30 ml) honey

FOR THE MERINGUES
4 egg whites, at room temperature

¼ tsp cream of tartar

3 tbsp (27 g) coconut sugar, divided

½ tsp almond extract

Preheat the oven to 225°F (107°C), and line a baking sheet with parchment paper.

For the strawberry sauce, stir together the strawberries and honey in a small saucepan. Cook the mixture over medium-low heat for 10 minutes, or until the strawberries start to become thick. Remove the sauce from the heat and let it cool completely.

For the meringues, with an electric mixer, beat the egg whites in a medium-sized mixing bowl until they become frothy. Add in the cream of tartar and continue beating. Add the sugar, 1 tablespoon (9 g) at a time, until all the sugar is incorporated and stiff peaks have formed. Stiff peaks are formed when you lift the beater and you get a peak that holds its shape. Fold in the strawberry sauce and almond extract.

Spoon the meringues, in 1½-inch (4-cm) dollops, onto the prepared pan, pulling your spoon up at the end to create a small swirl at the top.

Bake the meringues for 1 hour, or until they are crisp but not browned. If you can easily lift a meringue off the parchment, they are done. Turn off the oven and leave the meringues in the closed oven for at least 4 hours or up to overnight.

Store the meringues at room temperature in an airtight container.

PEACH CRUMBLE BARS

I don't make desserts often, and my friends and I have an inside joke about how I'm "not a dessert person." So, when I do make dessert, it better be darn good. I have a soft spot in my heart for some good ice cream and pie, and this peach crumble warms my heart. These bars are fresh, light and filled with healthy fats from the coconut. We love to enjoy this dessert warm from the oven, but the bars are a delight cold, too.

SERVES 8

FOR THE DOUGH
1 cup (112 g) superfine almond flour
1 cup (112 g) cassava flour
⅔ cup (96 g) coconut sugar
½ tsp baking soda
Pinch of salt
1 egg
¼ cup (60 ml) melted coconut oil
2 tbsp (30 ml) honey

FOR THE FILLING
4 fresh peaches, sliced
1 tbsp (15 ml) lemon juice
2 tsp (5 g) ground cinnamon
½ tsp ground nutmeg
1½ tbsp (12 g) arrowroot powder
2 tbsp (30 ml) honey
2 tbsp (5 g) chopped fresh basil, optional

FOR THE CRUMBLE TOPPING
½ cup (56 g) superfine almond flour
1½ tsp (4 g) ground cinnamon
⅓ cup (80 g) coconut oil
6 tbsp (54 g) coconut sugar
Pinch of salt

For the dough, preheat the oven to 350°F (177°C), and line a quarter sheet pan with parchment paper.

In a large bowl, use an electric mixer to combine the almond flour, cassava flour, sugar, baking soda and salt. Add the egg, coconut oil and honey to the flour mixture, and mix until dough forms. Press the dough evenly into the pan; put some cassava flour on your fingers if the dough is sticky. Poke holes with a fork into the dough and bake it for 10 minutes.

For the filling, in another mixing bowl, mix the peaches, lemon juice, cinnamon, nutmeg, arrowroot powder, honey and basil, if using, until the ingredients are well-combined. Pour the filling evenly into the parbaked dough.

For the topping, mix together the almond flour, cinnamon, coconut oil, sugar and salt until the mixture is crumbly. Sprinkle the topping evenly over the filling.

Return the pan to the oven and bake the bars for 20 minutes, or until the crumble topping is deep golden brown.

PALEO COFFEE CAKE

I have a confession: I don't like cake. When I was little, I always got pie with candles in it on my birthday! This Paleo Coffee Cake might have changed my mind, though. Not too sweet, the bars pair well with your morning coffee or evening tea.

SERVES 10–12

FOR THE CAKE

2 cups (224 g) superfine almond flour

⅓ cup (48 g) coconut sugar

1 tsp ground coffee

2 tbsp (16 g) tapioca flour

3 tsp (12 g) baking powder

½ tsp salt

1½ tsp (4 g) ground cinnamon

⅓ cup (80 ml) melted ghee

3 eggs

1½ tsp (8 ml) vanilla extract

FOR THE CRUMBLE TOPPING

¼ cup (28 g) superfine almond flour

¼ cup (28 g) tapioca flour

½ cup (72 g) coconut sugar

1½ tsp (2 g) ground coffee

3 tbsp (45 ml) melted coconut oil

Preheat the oven to 350°F (177°C), and line a quarter sheet pan with parchment paper.

For the cake, in a medium-sized mixing bowl, combine the almond flour, sugar, coffee, tapioca flour, baking powder, salt and cinnamon. Mix in the ghee, eggs and vanilla. Stir to combine the ingredients. Pour the batter—it will be a bit thick—onto your baking sheet and evenly spread it out.

For the topping, in a small bowl, mix together the almond flour, tapioca flour, sugar, coffee and coconut oil. Sprinkle half of the crumble topping over the batter.

Bake the coffee cake for 20 minutes, or until a toothpick inserted into the center comes out clean.

Remove the cake from the oven and let it cool in the pan for 5 minutes. Sprinkle the remaining half of the topping evenly over the top of the coffee cake, then cut it into bars. Serve warm.

SHEET PAN FRUIT PIZZA

This is a delightful and fresh Paleo sheet pan dessert to make on the weekend or for a small crowd. Play around with different fruits that are in season. I absolutely love this with strawberries and blueberries. It tastes magnificent with the Paleo-friendly vanilla custard.

SERVES 10

1½ tbsp (23 ml) melted coconut oil, for greasing

FOR THE DOUGH

2½ cups (280 g) superfine almond flour

¼ cup (36 g) coconut sugar

1 tsp baking powder

Pinch of salt

1 egg

¼ cup (60 ml) melted ghee

1 tsp vanilla extract

FOR THE VANILLA CUSTARD FILLING

1 (13.5-oz [398-ml]) can unsweetened full-fat coconut milk

1 cup (240 ml) unsweetened almond milk

½ cup (120 ml) honey

Pinch of sea salt

1 tbsp (15 ml) vanilla extract

1 tbsp plus 1½ tsp (11 g) unflavored gelatin

1 tsp vanilla bean seeds, optional

Sliced strawberries, peaches, nectarines, mangoes, bananas, blueberries, raspberries or a combination of fruits

For the dough, preheat the oven to 350°F (177°C), and grease a quarter sheet pan with coconut oil.

With an electric mixer, mix together the almond flour, sugar, baking powder and salt. Add the egg, ghee and vanilla, and mix until dough forms. Press the dough evenly into the prepared sheet pan. Using a fork, poke holes into the dough, then bake the dough for 10 minutes, or until the dough is set and golden brown.

To make the filling, in a pot over medium heat, whisk together the coconut milk, almond milk, honey, salt and vanilla. Sprinkle the gelatin over the milk as it is warming up. Whisk in the gelatin until it is completely dissolved and white foam forms on top of the mixture, about 2 minutes. Do not let the gelatin mixture come to a boil; reduce the heat, if necessary. Once the gelatin is completely dissolved, remove the pan from the heat, stir in the vanilla bean seeds, if using, and pour the custard over the cooked pizza dough.

Refrigerate the sheet pan pizza for at least 1 hour, or until the custard has set.

Top the custard with enough fruit to cover the pizza.

DELECTABLE STRAWBERRY SHORTCAKE

This Paleo-friendly strawberry shortcake is to die for! The great thing about this recipe is that most of your sweetness is coming from the super-fresh strawberries. Here's a little fun fact: Strawberries have the least amount of sugar of all fruit, with only about eight grams in eight strawberries. So, fill this delicious, low-sugar, Paleo shortcake up with all the strawberries!

SERVES 8–10

¾ cup (180 ml) melted coconut oil, plus 1½ tbsp (23 ml) for greasing

1½ cups (168 g) superfine almond flour

½ cup (56 g) cassava flour

⅔ cup (96 g) coconut sugar

2 tsp (8 g) baking powder

½ tsp sea salt

4 eggs

½ cup (120 ml) unsweetened full-fat coconut milk

1 tsp vanilla extract

Coconut cream, optional

2 cups (332 g) sliced strawberries

Preheat the oven to 350°F (177°C), and grease a quarter sheet pan with coconut oil.

In a large bowl, mix the almond flour, cassava flour, sugar, baking powder and salt. Crack the eggs into the flour, then add the melted coconut oil, coconut milk and vanilla, and mix until well-combined. Pour the shortcake batter onto the prepared pan.

Bake the shortcake for 25 minutes, or until a toothpick inserted into the center comes out clean. Let the shortcake cool in the pan for at least 5 minutes, then cut it into squares.

Because the shortcake is somewhat thin, I like to layer a piece of shortcake, followed by coconut cream, if using, strawberries, another piece of shortcake and more strawberries.

> **NOTE:** Coconut cream is now readily available at most natural grocery stores.

BAKED HASSELBACK APPLES WITH CARAMEL SAUCE

I love fall. The weather gets a bit cooler, but the best part is that it is apple season! Everyone always raves about pumpkins in the fall, but let's be real: Apples are where it's at. These Hasselback apples are great on their own, but the caramel sauce adds a certain *je ne sais quoi* to the dessert. The caramel sauce is made from coconut milk, which is a good source of healthy fats, and then drizzled over the apples, which are full of potassium and vitamin C.

SERVES 8

FOR THE CARAMEL SAUCE

1 (13.5-oz [398-ml]) can unsweetened full-fat coconut milk

½ cup (72 g) coconut sugar

Pinch of salt

½ tsp vanilla extract

FOR THE APPLES

¼ cup (60 ml) melted coconut oil, plus 1½ tbsp (23 ml) for greasing

4 medium apples, cored and halved vertically

1 heaping tbsp (8 g) ground cinnamon

Chopped walnuts, optional

For the caramel sauce, shake the can of coconut milk and pour the contents into a small saucepan. Whisk in the sugar, salt and vanilla and bring the mixture to a low boil. Reduce the heat to low, and simmer the sauce for 25 to 30 minutes, or until the sauce has reduced by half and is getting thick. Stir frequently throughout the simmering to prevent the sauce from burning on the bottom and sides of the pot. Remove the sauce from the stove, and let it cool.

Prepare the apples while the caramel sauce is cooling. Preheat the oven to 425°F (218°C), and grease a sheet pan with coconut oil.

Carefully make thin slices lengthwise on each apple half, but do not cut all the way through the apple. This is the Hasselback technique. Place the cut apples, open-side down, on the prepared pan. Brush the top of each apple with some of the coconut oil, then sprinkle cinnamon over the top. Lightly cover the apples with aluminum foil and bake them for 15 minutes. Brush more melted coconut oil over each apple. Re-cover and return the apples to the oven for another 15 minutes, or until the apples have softened.

For serving, drizzle some of the caramel sauce over the apples and top them with the walnuts, if using.

> **NOTE:** The caramel sauce will stay fresh in a glass jar in the refrigerator for up to 10 days. It will need to be stirred before each use.

THE FRUITIEST FRUIT ROLL-UPS

My mom used to make homemade fruit roll-ups in her dehydrator all the time, but it is very simple to make them in the oven. No fancy kitchen gadget needed! They are a great snack for your little ones—or you, if you don't have children. This recipe is the perfect alternative to the high-sugar, corn-syrupy and processed fruit roll-ups you find in the store. Have fun with flavors: Mix them up, even add some kale or spinach for a veggie-filled roll-up.

SERVES 12

FOR STRAWBERRY-PEACH ROLL-UPS

8 oz (227 g) strawberries

2 peaches, sliced

1 tbsp (15 ml) fresh lemon juice

FOR MANGO ROLL-UPS

3 mangoes, chopped

1½ tsp (8 ml) fresh lemon juice

FOR STRAWBERRY-APPLE-KALE ROLL-UPS

8 oz (227 g) strawberries

1 cup (224 g) unsweetened applesauce

1 cup (67 g) chopped kale

1 tsp fresh lemon juice

Preheat the oven to 170°F (76°C) (200°F [93°C] if your oven does not go as low as 170), and line a baking sheet with parchment paper.

For the strawberry-peach roll-ups, puree the strawberries and peaches in a blender until the mixture is smooth. Add the lemon juice, then pulse to blend it in.

For mango roll-ups, puree the mangoes in a blender until they are smooth. Add the lemon juice, then pulse to blend it in.

For the strawberry-apple-kale roll-ups, use a blender to puree the strawberries, applesauce and kale until the mixture is smooth. Add the lemon juice, then pulse to blend it in.

Spread the pureed fruit mixture ⅛ inch (4 mm) thick over the parchment paper in the prepared pan. If the puree is thicker, it will take longer to cook.

Bake the fruit mixture for a minimum of 3 hours, or until the fruit is no longer sticky to the touch.

Cool the mixture completely, then cut it—and the parchment paper under it—into 12 strips. Roll up the fruit with the parchment paper, and store the roll-ups at room temperature in an airtight container for up to 2 weeks.

ACKNOWLEDGMENTS

To Jenna Fagan, my editor at Page Street Publishing, who helped me create my first book baby. I will always be grateful. I hope we do more books together.

To everyone at Page Street Publishing working behind the scenes to make this book a reality: You are all amazing!

Thank you to the most amazing person I know, my mom, who taught me everything, showed me how to be a hard worker and was and has always been the best cheerleader.

Thank you to my amazing husband, Joe, who has been more supportive and patient than I could ever imagine. I love you too much. See you soon, "studio kitchen."

To my children, Joseph, Constance, Julian, Miles and Adelaide: You are my daily inspiration, and I love you all so much. Thanks for being patient through all the recipe-testing, picture-taking, Instagramming, etc. Work hard, dream big!

Thank you to all of my friends and family, for believing in me, supporting me and taste-testing all the recipes. Your love and encouragement have completely filled my heart box. If you know me, you know I'm not a hugger, but every one of you deserves the biggest hug.

To my fellow food bloggers (you know who you all are): Thanks for being a continuous source of inspiration and support. You are all the best cheerleaders and I'm honored to be surrounded by such wonderful, like-minded people who have become fantastic friends.

To my photographer Jerod Muse: This book would not be what it is without your stunning food pictures. You rock!

And last but not least, thank you to all my fans, followers and readers who continue to support me, enjoy the recipes I put out and laugh at my superb sense of humor.

ABOUT THE AUTHOR

Jennifer Bumb is the creator of the blog Pretend It's a Donut, where she shares Paleo, Whole30 and family-friendly recipes. Her recipes have appeared on Whole30.com and in *The Whole30 Cookbook* and have been featured in Whole Foods Market, Yummly, *Paleo Magazine* and HuffPost. She lives in San Jose, California, with her husband and five kids.

INDEX